BROOM.

LECTURES ON THE BOOK OF REVELATION

6. Oct 2008

Douglas & Margaret Broom.
"Pumula" Langford Rd.
Honiton Devon.

x

LECTURES ON
The Book of Revelation

J. Ritchie

JOHN RITCHIE LTD
CHRISTIAN PUBLICATIONS

40 Beansburn, Kilmarnock, Scotland

ISBN-13: 978 1 910513 03 3

Copyright © 2014 by John Ritchie Ltd.
40 Beansburn, Kilmarnock, Scotland

www.ritchiechristianmedia.co.uk

All rights reserved. No part of this publication may be reproduced, stored in a retrievable system, or transmitted in any form or by any other means – electronic, mechanical, photocopy, recording or otherwise – without prior permission of the copyright owner.

Typeset by John Ritchie Ltd., Kilmarnock
Printed by Bell & Bain Ltd., Glasgow

INTRODUCTION.

The Book of Revelation is by almost universal consent, among ordinary readers of the Bible, regarded as mysterious and difficult to understand. And for this reason they pass it by unread. Yet a special blessing is promised (Chap. i. 3) to all who "read" and "hear" and "keep" the inspired words of this Book, and a solemn judgment is threatened on all who despise or tamper with its contents (Chap. xxii. 18, 19). It is a part of the Sacred Scriptures against which the great Adversary holds and manifests a peculiar hatred, and little wonder, for it unveils and describes the coming glories of his Conquerer, the Lord Jesus Christ, and it records in clear and definite language his own discomfiture and downfall from the place that he now occupies as "prince of this world" (John xvi. 10), "god of this age" (2 Cor. iv. 4), and chief ruler of those wicked spirits under whose control is the present world darkness (Eph. vi. 12 R.V.), and opposition to all that is of God and under the Lordship of Christ on this earth.

Its Title. "The Revelation of Jesus Christ" (ver. 1), is the title given to this Book by the Spirit, —not "The Revelation of St. John the Divine" as the uninspired headline of the A.V. and the R.V. give it. "The disciple whom Jesus loved" assuredly received and wrote this Book, but the Revelation or Unveiling, is that of the Person of Jesus Christ. The word *Apocalypse*, which is sometimes used to designate it, signifies the rolling back of a veil so as to manifest an object hid. For the present, the glorified Lord is seated on the Father's throne, hid from the gaze of men. But the hour will come, when He will rise from that throne and His glory will be unveiled, first to His own, when they see Him as He is (1 John iii. 2), and behold the glory which has been given to Him by the Father (John xvii. 24), then to the world when He appears in glory with all His saints (Col. iii. 4), in the character described in Chap. xix. 11-15, to execute judgment on His foes, and cleanse ungodliness from the earth over which He is to rule as King and His saints with Him. It is of His coming thus of which the Revelation treats. His coming for His saints, with the raising of the dead in Christ and the change of the living, was part of a hidden mystery revealed to Paul, and by him communicated to the Church (1 Cor. xv. 51-54: 1 Thess. iv. 15-17). But the unveiling, or Epiphany of the Lord, as Son of Man, is that to which we are directed in this Book, and this is the testimony which is borne by the saints in ver. 7—"Behold He cometh with clouds and every eye shall see Him." His coming FOR His own is not described, save symbolically, in Chap. iv. 1-4, which is the point in the order of events at which it occurs, being at the close of the Church period as described in Chapters ii. iii., and before the Judgment period which begins in Chapter vi. and continues to Chapter xix., in which the Lord by judgment takes possession of the inheritance of which the title deeds are placed in His hand in Chapter v. This Epiphany of the Lord as Son of Man, will strike terror to the hearts of the great ones of the world, for they know full well that it brings their doom.

Its Divisions. The key to a right understanding of this Book lies at the door of it. It is found in ver. 19, in the threefold divisions there described: *First*, "The things which thou hast seen," which are comprised in the vision of verses 18-20, where the living Lord as Son of Man is seen in the midst of His Churches, under the symbol of golden lampstands. This is PAST. *Second*, "The things which are." These are recorded in Chapters ii. iii., in which the Church on earth is described in the seven stages of its history. This is PRESENT. *Third*, "The things which shall be hereafter"—or more correctly "after these," or "which are about to be after these." This third division is the prophetic part of the Book, extending from Chap. iv. to Chap. xxii. 9. This is wholly FUTURE, and includes the judgments of the Seals, Trumpets, Vials, the doom of Babylon and the Beast, the Millennial Kingdom of the Lord, and the final judgment. When these divisions are seen, and the whole Book read in their light, there will be no liability to mix together "things that differ," or to confuse the heavenly people and their hopes with things belonging to the earth, and the fulfilment of the purposes of God concerning His earthly people Israel in days to come.

Its Character. The teaching of this Book is, when used aright, as a "light shining in a dark place" (2 Pet. i. 19), casting the light of heaven on present conditions, alike on that which bears the name of God's Church and on the world, with principles at work in both, which will, when fully ripened, bring the Divine judgment upon them, the false Church being ultimately spued from the Lord's mouth in utter disgust, and the rebel world in the zenith of its godlessness being made to tremble under the power of His wrath, when once it is kindled. The varied forms of departure from God and His Word, even among true Christians, are here set forth, in order that the people of God, and especially the servants of Jesus Christ who represent Him and carry on His work during His absence, may be warned and instructed as to their path in the midst of these abounding corruptions. Divine Government, rather than grace, characterises this Book.

Its Message. It is not its business to record in detail the progress of evil during the past eighteen centuries of man's history, or to describe the leading actors therein, for in that case it would require to be a history of the world, but it does set forth in vivid and awful facts the climax of human iniquity, and the doom that awaits those who have had pleasure therein. The readers of this Book have no need to become acquainted with the history of the nations in order to understand its teaching, for the Lord has expressly told us that the Holy Spirit, who indwells all true believers, whom they have as an Unction to teach them all things (1 John ii. 27), has been given to guide them into all truth (John xvi. 13), so that they may learn and stand complete in all the will of God (Col. iv. 12), without going either to the world's newspapers, or to the history of the

Roman Empire, written by an infidel, to give them the necessary key to the symbols of this last Book of God's Bible. Had Christian expositors and teachers known and remembered this simple fact of the Spirit's ability and readiness to make known to the inquiring saint the "things of God," which He so well knows and has come for the very purpose of making plain to those who have eyes to see and ears to hear them (1 Cor. ii. 14), it would have saved them from the error of reading this Book of Revelation, in the flickering light of the lamp of secular history, and reading into the sacred symbolic language, events and actions of which it has nothing to say. For since the world rejected the Son of God, by putting Him on a felon's Cross (Acts iii. 14, 15), and the earthly people, of " whom as concerning the flesh Christ came" (Rom. ix. 5), refused the message of mercy sent by Him to them, from the throne upon which as Prince and Prophet He waited, ready to return to them as a repentant people (Acts iii. 19-26), wrath has come upon the Jewish people to the uttermost (1 Thess. ii. 16), and they have been left in their blindness as a nation (Rom. xi. 25), until the hour strikes when God shall resume His dispensational dealings with them. And upon the great Gentile world, whose rulers and nations are already in the beginning of the throes of their last great apostasy from God, as described in Psa. ii. 1-3, and even now seem to be consolidating their forces for the reception of Antichrist as their Kaiser and their God, there is nothing to be expected but judgment. Two things alone prevent it from falling now. First, that the Lord has not yet completed His present work of grace in taking out from the nations a people for His Name (Acts xv. 14). Second, the presence of part of that people yet in the world with the Holy Spirit in and with them, acting as "that which withholdeth" (2 Thess. ii. 6), hindering the full development of lawlessness and Satanic power by their presence. But when they go, which they will, all of them in "a moment," at the coming of the Son of God from heaven (1 Thess. i. 9), THEN, with the salt gone from the earth, and the light from the world, corruption will proceed without hindrance, and gross darkness will fall like a shroud upon the people—especially on those lands where the light of Truth has shone, only to be rejected—and the devil will be allowed to have his way, which his representative on earth will administer with Satanic deception upon men (2 Thess. ii. 9-12). It is the full development of this that the Revelation records, with the swift and final judgment of God upon it. Need we wonder, if the religious leaders of a worldly Christianity disregard or seek to obscure the Book that tells of these things, reading into its pages events of which it takes no notice whatever, using the very symbols given by God to warn of coming wrath for the exaltation of unregenerate man, and for the glorification of his religious systems and their ways. This, as we shall see, is what has been done by many who have taken upon themselves the task of expounding the Book of Revelation, according to their own fancies, and in the light of the world's history throughout the past eighteen centuries.

Interpretation. Three main schools of interpretation of this Book exist, mutually destructive of each other. 1. The *Preterist*, which regards the whole of the events of the prophetic visions of the Book to be already fulfilled. According to this class of expositors, the events represented in the seals, trumpets, and vials, have already come to pass, and the rising up of the Beast, the number of his name, and the fall of Babylon, are all to be found fulfilled in events of ancient history. This has the tendency to lower Divine Revelation to the level of a mere record of events, making human history the interpreter of the Bible. In this system there is no place for the distinct outcalling of the Church as the body of Christ or of the Churches as God's witnesses in separation from the world, while they are lights shining in it.

2. The *Presentist* or Historical interpretation gives to the history of the professing Church a large—one might say a too large—place in its scheme, but it fails to distinguish between "the Jew, the Gentiles and the Church of God" (1 Cor. x. 31), the three great classes into which mankind are divided. And the Year-day system which its interpreters adopt, is unwarranted in the Word, and necessitates a forced and unnatural construction being put on many passages, which in some instances amounts to "wresting the Scriptures." While there may be a *partial* fulfilment of many predictions, and the appearance of persons who in their deeds in measure answer to such yet future individuals as the Beast and the Antichrist of Rev. xiii., we do not admit that this is the *fulfilment* of the prophecy. And by finding events which are recorded in the section

which the Spirit describes as "the things which shall be *after* these," in the section which He calls "the things *which are*," there is confusion. God is a God or order, and when He states, as clearly He does, that the prophetic part of this Book does not begin to be fulfilled while the Church continues in the world, we do not expect to find events of the future transpiring in the present. 3. The *Futurist* school of interpretation places the whole of the visions and prophecies of this Book in the future: even the Seven Churches are made to represent Jewish Assemblies of the latter days. This gives no place at all to the "things which are," and the message to each hearing ear to hear "what the Spirit saith unto the Churches," can have no present message to the reader of the Book. This cannot stand, as it is contradictory alike of the Christian's proper hope and of the Church's present place as God's witness in the world. The right interpretation of the Book is to be found in a strict adherence to the threefold division as given by the Lord Himself in Chap. i. 19, then to the hearing ear and the waiting heart the Spirit will teach the meaning of the words He has caused to be written for the edification and help of the people of God, to whom this Book has been given as a Guide and a Lamp to direct their steps, and to show a "plain path" amid the perils and corruptions of these last days.

CHAPTER I.

SYNOPSIS:—The Title—The Symbols—The Subjects. The Seven Churches. The Divine Name—The Lord's Titles—The Song—The Testimony. The Exile in Patmos—The Lord's Day. The Vision—The Son of Man—Stars and Lampstands.

THE opening words of this Book express its character. They introduce us to the Lord Jesus under titles, and in a position, which we do not find Him occupying in earlier portions of the Word of God. In the Gospels we see Him as the Son declaring the Father, telling out His love, ever full of grace and truth, speaking that which He hears from the Father (John viii. 26). In the Epistles He is seen as exalted to the throne of God, the Lord and Leader of His people, Head of His body the Church, and Hope of all that believe. There all is grace, of which He is the Revealer and Pattern. Here, He is seen as the Administrator of Divine judgment, first in the midst of His Churches on earth, later in the world which has filled its cup of iniquity to the brim. The Book is "The (or a) Revelation of Jesus Christ which God gave unto Him." "Jesus Christ" is the Name by which John had known and believed in Him on earth (John xvii. 3), and occurs in this chapter only. He is not here seen in His essential

Deity, the Son in equality with the Father, knowing all His counsels, but as in His place as Executor of the Divine decrees as they are made known and given by Him who holds them in His own authority (see Acts i. 7, R.V.: with Mark xiii. 32).

The Divine Name. The Name "Jesus"–without prefix or affix—which means *Jehovah-saving* (Matth. i. 21), occurs in this Book nine times, and is heard from His own blessed lips in heavenly glory for the last time before the heavens become silent: "I Jesus, have sent Mine angel to testify unto you these things in the churches" (Chap. xxii. 16). As glorified Man, this Revelation comes to Him from "God," and it is given to Him in order that He may "show unto His bondservants the things which must shortly come to pass." It is not a "message" from the Father to His children, declared by this Apostle, as in his Epistle (1 John i. 3), in order to fellowship, but a revelation from God to those who as "bondservants" own His claims and authority, and stand girded to do His will on earth, after the manner of their great Exemplar, when He stood in the bondservant's form here among men (Phil. ii. 7). For it is to enlighten and to strengthen those who belong to Christ in their character as servants, owning Him as their Lord, that this Book has its practical value. To others, it will have but little interest. For if saints of God are mixed up in the world, conforming to its ways, sharing in its politics, and taking part in its religion, they will have neither ear to hear nor heart to heed the great things set forth in this Book.

The manner in which this "Revelation of Jesus

Christ" was communicated to His servant is peculiar. "He sent and signified it by His angel to His servant John." The apostles were not so instructed in the communications they were entrusted with for the Churches, to whom their epistles are addressed. Paul speaks of that which he had received of the Lord (1 Cor. xi. 23: xv. 3), direct from heaven (Gal. i. 13), but here an angel—one of that hierarchy, who are subjects of the glorified Lord (1 Pet. iii. 22), of whom we know so little—is employed as the medium of communication between Jesus Christ and John. This betokens distance, and is in striking contrast to the way John had learned His Master's will, as he reclined in His bosom in days of old (John xiii. 23, R.V.), and as he had the message given him to write to the family of God in his epistles (1 John i. 1-3). Here it is not Grace but *Government* that is in view, not sons but *servants* who are addressed, not the Father but *God* who gives the communication. All this strongly marks the character of the Book, and prepares us for lessons in God's school, which have reference to our place as His servants and witnesses in this world, in which His Christ has been rejected and from which He was cast out, rather than as children in His family sharing His love, and sons in His household partaking of His nature and dignity.

"The Word of God and the testimony of Jesus Christ" (ver. 2), surely includes "all things that he saw," the former being His counsels which He makes known, and the latter the announcement and administration of these counsels to the churches and the world by Jesus Christ.

Blessing is promised to the reader, the hearer, and those who keep—in the sense of observing (Matth. xxviii. 20), these communications—a blessing which none enjoy who neglect or fail to obey, what the Lord has here commanded. The reading may be private, in personal communion with God, with an ear upturned to hear His voice direct to the soul—a daily attitude (Psa. lxxxv. 8), of great value to the individual, but it probably has reference to the public reading of the Word which Paul charged Timothy to "give attendance to," in the assembly of the saints (1 Tim. iv. 13)—a practice which has sadly failed. "They that hear," seems to point to those congregated where the Word is thus read, and upon all the responsibility to "keep those things" is laid, in view of the fact that "the time is at hand." For while any theory of prophecy may be held as an intellectual asset, yielding no effect in the life, prophetic truth, rightly understood, is practical, and makes people act. This is why many do not like it. It was not that upon which all were agreed that God sent His prophets of ancient time to speak to His people, but to bring home to their consciences what they had neglected, and to declare to them their backslidden condition, with the chastisement and loss that it had brought upon them. This was not a popular ministry; it never will be.

The Salutation (ver. 4). The writer and the receivers of the Book having been named, the familiar salutation of "Grace and Peace" is given, in the Triune Name, yet not as in the Pauline epistles from Father, Son, and Spirit (2 Cor. xiii. 14), or from

"God our Father and the Lord Jesus Christ" (1 Cor. i. 3), but from *Jehovah*—the ever-existing One, "Him which is, which was, and which is to come"—the Name of majesty and power which none can claim but God. That it belongs to the Son in His exaltation (Phil. ii. 11), is a striking proof of His Deity.

"He sent and *signified* it by His angel to His servant John." The language of signs and symbols further reminds us that the Lord had, as in times when He spoke by parable (Matth. xiii. 13-15), withdrawn Himself from the mass of professors, and that His words were such that only the instructed ear would hear, and the exercised heart understand. For while lampstands and stars are symbolic figures, the things that they represent are existing realities, as the Lord Himself informs us (see chap. i. 20). John, to whom these communications were made, is neither addressed as apostle or ecclesiastic, but simply as "His servant, John," who, while severed from the churches in which the years of his active ministry were spent, is still filling that honoured place. He neither here nor elsewhere, makes any claim to the high office and loud-sounding titles with which tradition associates his name. It was enough for him, while closing his Gospel, to introduce himself only as "the disciple which testifieth of these things" (John xxi. 24), and here as "I John who saw these things, and heard them" (Chap. xxii. 8). It is happy with the servant of the Lord when he is able to keep the place to which He has been appointed, and on all occasions to honour his Lord, effacing himself.

"The seven Spirits which are before the throne," present a new aspect of the one Holy Spirit with whom we are familiar in the Epistles, as the Comforter, who abides in and with the saints throughout this age of grace, who forms the body of Christ (1 Cor. xii. 13), and indwells the Church as God's temple (1 Cor.iii.16), and habitation (Eph.ii.22). But here the Spirit is "before His throne" in a sevenfold plenitude of His power, not occupied in gathering a people out from the world by the Gospel (Acts xv. 14: 1 Thess. i. 5), or in guiding (John xvi. 13), and strengthening (Eph. iii. 16), those who have been already quickened by His power into new life, and sealed by Him for heavenly glory (Eph. i. 13). The work appointed to the Spirit in the age to come is connected with government administered from heaven on earth, in grace and in judgment, in which the Spirit, as many Old Testament Scriptures teach us, will have a special and far-reaching part (see Isa. xl. 7: Zech. xii. 10: Ezek. xxxvii. 14: Joel ii. 28), in preparing a people on the earth for the Lord, and in working among them all that will be needed to sustain the testimony they will be called to bear suited to the time in which they live, and in controlling all things, as He is directed from the throne of God. All this is to be distinguished from the Spirit's present place and operations. The salutation is also from "Jesus Christ," here named after the Spirit, which points to another relation than the present age, in which the Spirit which proceedeth from the Son (John xv. 25), is given only to "them that obey Him" (Acts v. 32), and seals only such as believe (Eph. i. 13). The

Spirit will, in the period of "the things which shall be after these," be the attendant of the throne of God, and will operate according to the outworking of His counsels in His dealings with earth. Thus He is to be found in other relations than the present. "Grace," which includes all gifts and blessings, with "peace," which sets and keeps the heart at ease before God, give the right condition and supply for all service, ever keeping the servant in constant touch with, and in continuous dependance upon God.

Three Titles, which belong to the Lord Jesus alone, are next named in their due order. "THE Faithful WITNESS" has reference to His path and testimony here on earth in the *Past*. To "bear witness unto the truth" (John xviii. 37), was His business in the world, and He did it faithfully and perfectly, never flinching, never faltering, fearing no frown, seeking no praise from man. He is the only One who stood wholly for God here. "FIRST-BORN of the dead," first in rank, views Him in the *Present*, beyond death in resurrection, as well as Forerunner and pledge of the final glory of all His people. Because He lives they shall live also. "PRINCE of the Kings of the earth" looks on to the *Future*, to the time when "all kings shall fall down before Him" and "all nations shall serve Him" (Psa. lxxii. 11). All authority has already been given Him (Matth. xxviii. 18), but "we see not *yet* all things put under Him" (Heb. ii. 8). But His sovereign rights will yet be exercised, and all will own them, proud emperors, kings, and rulers bowing at His feet as their Prince and Supreme Ruler.

A Doxology. The announcement of the Lord in this threefold glory, brings at once a song of praise from the redeemed on earth. The language of the song tells who the singers are, for none in heaven or on earth can sing such a song but the Church, basking in the full revelation of Christ's love as manifested in the Cross, standing in the virtue of the blood there shed for her redemption. "Unto Him who loveth us, and loosed us from our sins by His blood" (R.V.), tells of the heart won, the bonds broken, the conscience free, and the soul at rest. These are mercies common to all the saints: they are theirs by grace alone. Yet how few stand in their constant enjoyment with hearts uplifted in the praise of the eternal Lover, who loved, and loveth, and will love His own to "the end" (John xiii. 1).

This song of the redeemed on earth is the same in character as the song to be sung by the glorified in heaven (Chap. v. 10). Nor is the love of His heart and the freedom procured by His blood the whole, for other blessings, the results of the Cross, immediately follow. "He made us to be a kingdom, priests unto His God and His Father" (R.V.). "Hath made us a sovereignty," expresses the truth better, for the thought here is not that the saints are to be governed by the One whose supreme authority over all has just been announced, but that His sovereign authority has been conferred upon them, which they shall exercise with Him when He reigns. "Priests unto God" tells what all saints of the present age have individually already been "made," for it is of them that the apostle writes: "Ye *are* a chosen generation, a royal priesthood, a holy nation" (1 Pet. ii. 9). To exercise the functions of this priesthood in drawing near to God (Heb. x. 22), in offering up "spiritual sacrifices" (1 Pet ii. 5), and in "worshipping God by the Spirit" (Phil. iii. 3, R.V.), are privileges of all saints—not of any sacredotal or set apart circle among them, who, claiming special rights, say to others—"Stand by, for I am holier than thou" (Isa. lxv. 5). For the blood which gives the title (Heb. x. 19), and the indwelling Spirit who gives the competency (Col. i. 12), avail for all the redeemed, and their value is to be appropriated and used by them. "Sovereignty," although already theirs, is not for the present in exercise: they await for that hour in which the "Sovereignty" of the world (Chap. xi. 15), shall pass into the hands of their once-rejected Lord, and when He reigns, "when He sits as King-Priest on His throne" (Zech. vi. 13), His heavenly people will reign also. To reign now, and to be exalted where He was rejected, and His faithful followers are accounted as "refuse" (1 Cor. iv. 13, R.V.), is not an evidence of advanced spiritual attainment, but of carnality and babyhood in Divine things (1 Cor. iii. 1). The ascription, "to whom be the glory, and dominion, for ever—to the ages of ages," expresses the desire of the saints that all that is foretold of "glory"—and there is much, and all that is foreshadowed of "dominion," great and far-reaching (see (Psa. lxxii. 8, 17: Isa. xxxii. 1), shall be Christ's, which 1 Pet. v. 11 tells us they shall. The "Amen" is not here "Let it be," but is the Lord's "Verily, verily," that thus it shall be.

A Prophetic Testimony. The song and ascription is followed by a solemn testimony to the world. "Behold, He cometh with clouds, and every eye shall see Him" (ver. 7). This has no reference to the coming of the Son of God to the air FOR His people, but to the coming of the Son of Man WITH His own in judgment, to the earth, as Dan. vii. 13 and Matth. xxiv. 30 describe it. His manifestation in majesty and glory, will strike terror to the ungodly, whose eyes shall then see Him, who was last seen by the world on a felon's Cross of shame. What a sight this will be! How sinners will quail before the brightness of His appearing, as they wither and perish at His glance! "They also which pierced Him," views Israel in "that day" when they look on Him, their own Messiah, whom they in the time of their blindness and unbelief "pierced," but now by grace repentant they mourn for Him as one that is in bitterness for His first-born (Zech. xi. 10). And "all the tribes"—the two then in their land and the ten on the way to it —"shall wail" in the "great mourning" of that day, which will lead them to the "fountain opened," there to learn that in virtue of the atoning death of the Lamb of God, who was wounded for their transgressions, they are "clean from all their sins before the Lord" (Lev. xvi. 30). Of this their great atonement day of ancient time was the foreshadowing type. But the "wail" will extend to Gentiles in all lands, not in repentance as in awakened Israel, but in abject fear, for they know that the day of the Lord thus coming upon them, "as a thief in the night" (1 Thess. v. 2), brings their doom. This is our testimony to the world, as it was Enoch's, five thousand years ago (Jude 14). Let it be loud and clear and ringing, sealed as it will be by the double "Even so, Amen," of the Spirit, for all that God has spoken will assuredly come to pass. "Alpha and Omega"—the first and last letters of the Greek alphabet—He is Beginning and End, Originator and Fulfiller of all that He has planned and uttered. "Jehovah"—the Everlasting One, combining past, present, and future in one word; and because He is "the Almighty,"—God All-sufficient, He is well able to do it, and no power on earth or in hell can hinder it. With this mighty word of power the introduction closes.

The Vision of John. We now approach the great vision given to the Seer, who first gives in brief words his position and his commission. "I John, your brother and partaker with you—joint-partaker—in the tribulation and kingdom and patience in Jesus" (ver. 6, R.V.),—one in calling and state with those to whom he writes, their representative and fellow-partaker. "In the tribulation;" this had been promised by the Lord (John xvi. 33), and the measure of it as "much" repeated by the apostle (Acts xiv. 22). Tribulation* was and is

---

*"The tribulation" here, is not to be confused with the "great tribulation," more literally "the tribulation, the Great one" of Chap. vii. 14, which belongs to the "things which shall be after these," and will take place during the latter part of Daniel's seventieth week. Those who "come out of" it are not Christians of the present age, but "an innumerable multitude" out of all nations, who in the time of Antichrist's reign of terror stand true to God. Their faithful testimony is owned in heaven, for they are made to share millennial bliss.

the common lot of all who belong to Christ (Rom.
v. 3), as they are being educated for their places in
the glory to be revealed. Already in the kingdom
of the Son (Col. i. 13), with foes around, they must
endure hardness, for it is not yet the day of "the
kingdom and glory" (1 Thess. ii. 12), to which they
are called. The King is still rejected on earth, and
those who are to reign with Him must "suffer" now
(2 Tim. ii. 12), unless they choose to shirk the cross
and miss the crown (Rev. iii. 11), which is the more
popular and pleasing path. But "the patience in
Jesus" is that to which all His own are called,
following in the steps of Him who "endured the
cross, despising the shame" (Heb. xii. 2), with "the
joy set before Him" full in view.

Patmos. "The isle called Patmos"—a rocky islet
of the Ægean Sea, some 15 miles in circumference,
formerly named *Palmosa* because of its palms,
which long have perished, now *Patino*, bare, in-
hospitable, and lone. It had become the place of
John's exile, whither he had in all likelihood been
banished as a criminal, by either Nero or Domitian,
who were cruel persecutors of the Christians. Here
John the beloved, the last survivor of the twelve,
now far advanced in years, learned the meaning of
that word of His Lord, spoken in answer to his
mother's request, that he and his brother James
might have the places of chief honour in sitting on
the right and left hand of the Lord in the day of
His kingdom. To this the answer came "Ye shall
drink indeed of My cup, and be baptized with the
baptism that I am baptized with" (Matth. xx. 23).
James, "the brother of John" (Acts xii. 2), had be-

come the victim of Herod's sword at least fifty years before, and now John the Aged, who had leaned on the bosom of the Lord in the upper room, and stood close by the side of His Cross (John xix. 26), in the last hour when others had forsaken him and fled, is honoured in being exiled for "the Word of God and the testimony of Jesus" to this lone isle, which had become his sanctuary. Not a word of complaint is heard of his hard lot, nor any call for vengeance on his unjust judges. Tradition has much to tell of his condemnation and his life on Patmos, but all is legend. The simple statement, "I was in the isle called Patmos," is all that the exile has given us, and no matter what the accusation in the records of the Roman court under which John was sentenced, the true cause is recorded in heaven's undying chronicles as being "for the Word of God and the testimony of Jesus." And although times are changed, and persecution now assumes other forms, the world will still show its hostility to the man who stands firm for that "Word," and who gives a certain sound in that "testimony."

The Lord's Day. Far from the scenes of his happy early years on the shores of the Lake, where he first met the Lord and heard His voice (Mark i. 19, 20), and from the fields of labour in which he had spent the years of his vigour in preaching the Word (Acts iv. 13), and watching over the newly-gathered churches (Acts viii. 14), throughout the Roman earth, John is no longer privileged to assemble with fellow-saints as had been his wont on "the first day of the week" (Acts

xx. 7), with the Lord Himself in the midst. But no power of earth or hell could hinder the living Lord from drawing near to His exiled saint, and giving him such sights of the glories that await the redeemed as had never before been revealed to man on earth. And not for himself alone, but that he might "write" of the "things that he had seen," to cheer and uplift and gladden the hearts of saints in all the ages. It seems to be God's way to permit His servants to become prisoners and exiles, in order that He may speak to them in secret that which they shall minister to thousands. Luther, a prisoner in the Wartburg, translated the Bible; Bunyan, in Bedford Jail, wrote the *Pilgrim's Progress;* Rutherford, in his "Prison Palace," at Aberdeen, wrote his Letters full of Christ and bright with the "glory that dwelleth in Immanuel's Land." On a certain "Lord's Day" John became in [the] Spirit. This is something more than is common to Christians now. Every true believer in Christ is "in the Spirit" (Rom. viii. 9), as to his standing before God, and "in the Spirit" also in his life (Gal. v. 25). It was his and is our proper state also to have the Spirit indwelling (1 Cor. ii. 12: vi. 19), and to be full of (Acts vi. 5: xi. 24), and filled with the Spirit (Acts iv. 31: Eph. v. 19). But this reference of John is more. As Paul had been "caught up" into the heaven to see and hear unspeakable things, so John "became in the Spirit." He was for the time being on that particular Lord's Day, withdrawn from the course of ordinary Christian life, raised to a state higher even than that fellowship with the Father and the Son (1 John i. 3) that he knew so well, into an estactic state, held so in the grasp of the Spirit that all that he saw was a Divine unveiling, and all that he heard was the voice of the Lord. It is vain for any to claim such a condition now, for the Word being completed, there is nothing to add to it. All that God intended us to know has been written, and those who claim to have "revelations" and "manifestations" from heaven are either deceived or wilfully deceivers of those whose confidence they seek.

Some have intrepreted this expression "the Lord's Day" to mean "the day of the Lord" (1 Thess. v. 2: 2 Pet. iii. 10), and regard the whole of the events to follow, including those of Chapters ii. iii., to belong to it. But this cannot stand. For the expression "the Lord's Day" is entirely different from "the day of the Lord," so frequently found in both Old and New Testaments. The word used occurs just twice; here and 1 Cor xi. 20, in connection with the Lord's Supper, the one to distinguish it from a common meal, the other to fix the day on which it is to be celebrated. The Lord's Supper has been the memorial of Christ's death: the Lord's Day the witness of His resurrection, all through the ages. Both belong to and are claimed by the Lord, in the seal of His Name being put upon them. He honoured the first Lord's Day by taking His place in the midst of His own (John xx.). And in sending the Comforter, and beginning the Church (see Lev. xxiii. 16 with Acts ii. 1), at Pentecost, on another "Lord's Day." John, on that memorable Lord's Day, alone in Patmos, heard behind "a great voice as of a trumpet," giving clear and intelligible sounds to the ear trained to hear it. It was "behind" him, for what it had to communicate was first regarding things of time, while John, in his estactic state, had his eye fixed on the future.

The Written Roll. The words, "I am Alpha and Omega," repeated in ver. 11, are regarded as without authority, being possibly copied by some scribe from ver. 8, and it was not till John "turned to see the Voice that spake" (ver. 12), that the Speaker, and who He is, was revealed. "What thou seest write in a book—or roll—and send it to the Seven Churches." That roll, when completed, would be passed around the Seven Assemblies, whose names are given by the Lord. It contained not only the message which belonged to each particular assembly, but all were allowed to read the message of the Lord to the whole. Thus were they informed of His estimate of their own condition for self-judgment, humiliation, and rectification, and likewise of His judgment of others for their guidance in their attitude toward them. For whatever the Lord has to say about a Church, its doctrine, and its practice, should surely be the rule to regulate the relations and service of others toward it.

The Seven Churches. The names, Ephesus, Smyrna, Pergamos, Thyatira, Sardis, Philadelphia, Laodicea, are seven cities in which there were Assemblies of saints. The term "in Asia" does not mean the great continent bearing that name, nor yet the region, which about the fourth century received the name of Asia Minor, but a strip of it along the western seaboard, known as Pro-consular Asia, of which Ephesus was the capital. This was the "Asia" in which *all* its dwellers heard the Word of the Lord (Acts xix. 10) from Paul, and concerning which the silversmiths alleged that "almost throughout *all* Asia" (ver. 26), Paul had "turned away much people" from the worship of their idols. It was in these parts that the apostle spent "long time" preaching, and in which, part of the saints to whom Peter wrote, were found (1 Pet. i. 1).

Seven Golden Lampstands. John having turned to see, beheld seven Golden Lampstands—not candlesticks* as in the A.V., which we are informed in verse 20, are symbolic of the Seven Churches, whose names are given, and of the whole Church throughout the dispensation in testimony, during the present night of the world's history. It is not here the Church as the Body of Christ, formed in the Spirit (1 Cor. xii. 13), composed of all believers of the present dispensation, one with Christ and each other, to be presented intact and without blemish to the Lord by the Spirit at His return, but the Church in testimony, in any locality, in responsibility to God there, supplied with all that is needed to shed forth a heavenly light in the darkness around, by the indwelling Spirit of God (1 Cor. iii. 16), watched over by the living Lord in heaven. A Golden Lampstand had once stood in the Holy Place of the ancient tabernacle, with seven lamps of gold branching out from and supported

---

* A Candlestick holds a candle, which, when it is lit, gives light without care. A Lampstand is to uphold a Lamp into which fresh oil is poured, and which requires trimming. The latter is the emblem of the Church as filled with the Spirit, God's light-bearer on earth.

by a central stem, whose beauty was shown by the light that shown from these lamps of gold, daily filled and trimmed by Israel's priest. It symbolised the Church in union with Christ, filled with the Spirit, exhibiting the beauties of Christ glorified to the worshipping priests in the Holy Place. Here the lampstands are out in the dark world, each on its own base, yet all supplied with the same holy oil, their lamps watched over by the same Eye and trimmed by the same Hand. And in the midst of these seven lampstands, "One like unto the (a) Son of Man" is seen walking, as it were on a visit of inspection, to see whether they are fulfilling the purpose for which they had been set up on earth.

That there were seven actually existing Assemblies in that part of Asia, found in the varied spiritual conditions described by the Lord, and that these seven messages, committed to writing by John, were primarily to them, there can be no doubt. But that there is a wider application to these messages is equally clear. The word "mystery" in verse 20, would otherwise have no meaning, and the selection of these seven—which is the number of *completeness*—points to the fact that these churches, selected by the Lord, represent the whole course of the church on earth, viewed as God's witness, from Apostolic times to the Coming of the Lord, not as men view it, but as it is seen and judged by the Lord who searcheth all hearts. *Gold* is the most precious metal, and in symbolic language expresses that which is Divine. The Church is God's, not man's. It is of His creation, founded on the one foundation of His Son. Its constitution and order is according to His pattern (1 Cor. iii. 10-11); its testimony is to His person and work (1 Tim. iii. 15, 16). Like all else in which human responsibility has a place, it is subject to decline and corruption, and if unfaithful may be removed (Chap. ii. 5), although the saints who compose it can never forfeit their place "in Christ" (Eph. i. 3), nor in His body (Eph. v. 30).

The Vision of Christ. It was not to the seven cities of Asia, in which these churches had their actual existence, that John was carried "in Spirit," but to a heavenly scene in which the living Lord, robed in the garments of the Sanctuary, walked in the judicial aspect of His priesthood, discerning and judging the state of these churches. The name He bears is that which He is known by as Judge (John v. 22-27). The "Ancient of Days" in Daniel's vision (Dan. vii. 9), is similarily described. The ROBE, which He wears "down to the foot" (ver. 15), is the priestly ephod. In Aaron's garments it was all of blue—the heavenly colour. His GIRDLE—not worn around the loins, but "about the breasts," is golden also, and expresses the character of His service as faithfulness in love (see Isa. xi. 5, with Rev. iii. 19). "His HEAD and His hairs were white as wool," here, not symbolic of old age or decay, but of wisdom in purity and perfection. "His EYES as a flame of fire," searching out all hidden things, penetrating to the causes and motives which underlie actions and ways seen by man. "His FEET like fine (white) brass burning (glowing) in a furnace"—treading in judgment all that is evil, here in His churches and shortly in the world. "His VOICE was as the sound of many waters." The Voice that once stilled the angry waves of the Lake of Galilee, that spake "peace" to countless troubled hearts on earth, speaks now in majesty and power, "mightier than the noise of many waters" (Psa. xciii. 4), bringing all into subjection, to "stand in awe" at His Word (Psa. cxix. 161). "His COUNTENANCE was as the sun shineth in his strength"—on which no mortal eye can gaze —the Central Sun from which all lesser orbs receive their light, around which they all revolve. On earth His *moral* glory was manifested in His acts and deeds. This is what John refers to when He says "We beheld His glory" (John i. 14). His Divine glory was for the most part veiled, only glimpses of it here and there appearing, as *on* the Mount (Luke ix. 29). "The glory of God" now shines in "the face of Jesus Christ" (2 Cor. iv. 6), and to Paul, on the day of his conversion, it appeared as a light "above the brightness of the sun" (Acts xxvi. 13). Thus is the living Lord revealed in the office of His official priesthood, the same Person as John had known on earth, and followed through Judea and Galilee. Yet how different as here unveiled! For just as the Lord appeared in one form to Mary in the garden, and "in another form" (Mark xvi. 12), to the two travellers on the Emmaus road, so does He manifest Himself to His own according to their condition, and reveal Himself as the One suited to meet their need. In the Gospels, no description of the Lord in His physical form is given, nor should any in the form of prints or images be accepted or used by Christians. The Bride in the Song describing her Beloved (Chap. v. 10-16), gives in symbolic language the expression of a heart in communion with the Lord, as it finds Him spiritually to be, and here to the Seer, He stands revealed in His official character among His Churches. But only when His saints behold Him in resurrection beauty, themselves having been made like Him, shall they "see Him as He is" (1 John iii. 2). "Having in His HAND seven stars," which are said in ver. 20 to represent "the angels of the seven churches," telling of the living Lord as the holder and giver of all gifts of spiritual ministry, in whose right hand there is power to sustain what He provides. "Out of His MOUTH proceedeth a sharp two-edged sword." This is the Lord's use of the Word in its "piercing" and searching power *now* among His own (Heb. iv. 12), as it will be in another form among His foes on a coming day (Rev. xix. 15).

The effect of the vision on John is overwhelming. He falls "at His feet as dead." Once before, in the presence of His glory on the Mount, the hand of the transfigured Lord had "touched" him in the moment of His fear. Here the "right hand" of the glorious One is "laid upon" the aged "disciple, whom Jesus loved," lying at His feet, and the familiar reassuring word "Fear not" comes from His lips, with the assurance that He is "the First and the Last," ever the same, in Whom time and conditions work no change, the same Eternal Lover on whose bosom John had reclined in the upper room. He is seen now as glorified Man in heaven. "The Living One"—in whom Life ever was and is

c

(1 John i. 3), but who for our sakes "became dead" of His own will (John x. 18), and through death became death's Conqueror; now "alive for evermore" —to the ages of ages—Victor over him who once had death's power. He holds the "keys of Death and of Hades" (R.V.), having the right and authority of both, able to bring the bodies of His own from death's domain at His call, and their souls from Hades, the *Unseen*, where before His death they had been detained. Now they are in paradise (Luke xxiii. 43), awaiting the hour of final reunion.

The Angels. In the closing words of the commission to John to write, the seven stars in the Lord's right hand are said to be "the angels of the seven churches." Great controversy exists as to what the ecclesiastical standing of these "angels" is: cardinal, archbishop, minister, and elder each laying claim in turn to the word. These "stars" are seen in the Lord's hand, security and support being theirs from Him. They shine in the dark, this is their service. They are angels—messengers, this is their office. "Angels" are also representatives, as Matth. xviii. 10 tells us, and Acts xii. 15 illustrates. The "angels of the churches" would be the symbolical representatives of their condition, as well as the messengers of the Lord among them: in short those who serve and those who guide. Men who minister to and are leaders of an Assembly, whether few or many, are its responsible representatives, and what they are, as a rule, it is. But the fact that "the angel," and not—as in Paul's Epistles—the churches themselves are addressed, tells, that there has been departure from Christ, and

THE ANGEL OF THE CHURCH

this means that He adopts to reach them is the witness of it. But while this is so, the responsibility of all remains, for the messages, while sent to the "angels," are "what the Spirit saith unto the Churches."

Having elsewhere dealt with the Seven Churches in their Historic and Prophetic aspect, I do not intend to go into the details of each of the seven messages in that light now. But inasmuch as these two chapters form a fitting prelude to the "things that shall be after these," as described in Chapters iv.-xix., and set forth the beginnings of the evils in that which claims to be God's churches—His public testimony in the world—which will have their full development in the age which follows the present, bringing down the condign vengeance of heaven upon the whole scene in which Christendom has for ages corrupted herself with the nations, and dishonoured the Name of Him whom she calls her Lord—they require to be considered in this connection. Thus it will be seen that the germs of all those evils which will in the days of their fruition bring God's judgments on the earth, are already at work in the midst of those who are professedly "not of the world." And the judgment of the Lord as here recorded, tells the story of how the evil began, and the means used by the enemy for its development. This gives a solemn character to these messages, and ought to have the effect of bringing all who "have an ear to hear" them, into personal self-judgment before Him, who walks "in the midst," from whose eyes there is nothing hid.

CHAPTER II.

SYNOPSIS:—The Seven Messages. EPHESUS: Love and Labour—Love's Decline—The Apostolic Age. SMYRNA: Persecution and Suffering—The Pagan Pesecutions. PERGAMOS: The Church allied to the World—"Satan's Throne"—Constantine's Day. THYATIRA: The World ruling the Church—Jezebel and her Children—The Papal Period.

THERE are at least four ways in which the Seven Messages may be read and used by all Christian readers. *First*, the *Individual:* each word from the Lord being received and allowed to operate as a distinct and personal message to the heart and conscience. This is what is surely implied in the seven times repeated words "*He* that hath an ear to hear, let *him* hear." Listening to the solemn utterances of the living Lord thus, cannot fail to bring the "blessing" promised in Chapter i. 3 to the individual soul, whether others hear or not.

Second, the *Collective:* each assembly taking the words as applicable to itself and judging its condition, spiritual, doctrinal, and moral, in their light. Thus read and received as that which "the Spirit saith to the Churches," each assembly may discover its true state and act accordingly.

Third, the *General:* the Seven Churches representing the condition of all God's Churches on earth at any given period, some declining, others repentant and returning. Viewed thus, these chapters serve as a Spiritual thermometer, which when used aright allows all to find out where they are in relation to the Lord and His standard.

Fourth, the *Historic*, in which as in panoramic order, the Lord, who knows the end from the beginning, sets forth the entire course of the Church on earth, in the place of testimony, from Pentecost to His Parousia, giving beforehand the various devices of the enemy by which it would be corrupted and led into alliance with the world, to be finally rejected and utterly disowned by Him, a faithful remnant—including all His own—in each being promised special blessing and reward as "overcomers."

The first three and the last four, stand in separate groups. The call "he that hath an ear" in the message to Ephesus, Smyrna, and Pergamos, comes *before* the word and the promise to the overcomers (see verses 7, 11, 17: while in the messages to Thyatira, Sardis, Philadelphia, and Laodicea, they follow *after*, the one with the hearing ear being directed to the coming of the Lord as his hope, and not to a former condition as the others had been. For since the Church became amalgamated with the world, and Popery ruled it in the name of the Church, reformation for the mass has been impossible; but a faithful remnant is recognised in each of the four last conditions, which *all* continue to the end. So that we shall find Popery, Protestantism, Loyalty to Christ, and Religious Pretension going on side by side, until the Lord comes to sever the precious from the vile. All this is searching and solemn, and ought surely to awake in the hearts of all true lovers of the Lord the deepest interest in these seven last communications from Him, whom we call our Lord. The very next we shall hear from Him will be His "shout" when He comes into the lower heavens, to summon His own from the world to meet Him in "the air."

Succession. In the first three church periods, one succeeded another, the character of Ephesus passed, to be replaced by Smyrna, and that of Smyrna by Pergamos; but when we reach the fourth, as represented in Thyatira, this ceases. For while Sardis follows Thyatira, it does not cancel it; Popery continues alongside of Protestantism, and will continue to the end. But for the first time a faithful remnant is recognised (Chap. ii. 24), to which alone the promise is addressed, and not to the whole church. And instead of a general call to repentance, and a return to the original condition "from whence" they had fallen, the "overcomers" are directed to "hold" what they have in view of the Lord's coming—which truth is not directly named in the first three messages—as their goal and hope amid increasing failure and corruption.

Titles. The character in which the Lord presents Himself to each church, is just that which is suited to its condition, and the Titles He gives to Himself reveal such attributes as they need to apprehend in Him, as the One to whom they owe their existence, and of whose testimony they are the bearers among men.

Overcomers. The Seven Promises to the overcomers are so connected and continuous, that they cannot fail to conform the prophetic character of these messages. That the Seven Churches chosen by the Lord out of all then existing, with Himself walking in the midst, are intended to represent the continuous history of that which bears His Name throughout the whole of the present church age, there are abundant proofs, of which this is one. These promises include the seven great privileges all forfeited by man's disobedience, in times before the Cross, restored in character, but vastly increased in glory, corresponding in their order to that which had been lost through sin, all held forth as to be bestowed by the Lord to "overcomers," in the midst of the conditions in which their lot is cast. The Tree of Life views man's innocence in Eden: the Second Death refers to his fallen condition when death entered and "hurt" all mankind (Rom. v. 12): the Hidden Manna, recalls Israel's sin in the wilderness: the promise of Power to rule to the time of the Judges, who acted for God as individuals when the nation failed: the Priestly Robe of white, and the inscribed Name, call to mind the failure of the Aaronic priesthood, who, because of defilement, had their names removed from the register of that priesthood: the Pillar in the temple, to Solomon's reign of glory, followed by its ruin, and the "going out" of the land to Babylon: the sitting on Christ's Throne, to the glory and the throne once parted as in Ezekiel x. 1-4, and Dan. i. 1, to be restored and reunited in Christ in heavenly glory. Thus the path of faithfulness here, in the midst of increasing corruptness, will have a corresponding recompence "from glory to glory " there. And these blessings are possessed and enjoyed in a progressive order. At death, or when he falls asleep, the Christian enters Paradise (Luke xxiii. 43). The Crown of Life is awarded at Christ's Coming (Rev. xii. 1-2): The White Stone at His judgment-seat (2 Cor. v. 10): Power over the Nations: appointments for the Millennial Kingdom (Rev. xx. 6): Confessed before His Father at its zenith (Matth. xiii. 43), and close (1 Cor. xv. 28): the Name of the New Jerusalem written at the beginning of the Eternal State (Rev. xxi. 2): while the seventh and final, of being seated with Christ on His own throne (Rev. xxii. 3), looks on to His eternal Kingdom (2 Pet. i. 11). The present and personal application of all this to the people of God is of the greatest value to them, and the right use of it in an exercised heart, will lead to a godly and obedient life down here.

The Church in Jerusalem, while it was the first and in some respects the brightest in its testimony (see Acts ii. 44-47 : iv. 32-36), is not included in the Seven. Its light had early waned, and it had disappeared in the destruction that fell on the city before the time that this Revelation of Jesus Christ was given. Churches gathered from among the Gentiles are only viewed in these Chapters. These characterise the dispensation.

Ephesus. The city of Ephesus, known as the "Light of Asia," was the Capital of that Roman province in John's day. It was a seat and centre of idolatry, from which it spread far and wide. The great temple of Diana was there, and accounted one of the seven wonders of the world. Strangers from all parts visited it, and "the silversmiths," who made and sold small shrines of the goddess, which were carried home and worshipped as family deities, were a powerful body, as Acts xix. informs us. Into this citadel of Satanic power, Paul carried the Gospel (Acts xviii. 1-8: xix. 8-20), and a mighty work of grace was wrought, resulting in the formation of an assembly of believers, henceforth called "the Church" (ver. 17), "the flock" and "the Church of God" (ver. 28). There is every indication that in numbers it was large, in spiritual condition devoted, and that it had a clean and clear testimony at its beginning. For three years, Paul had personally laboured "night and day" in its midst, by word and example setting the ways of Christ before the saints. His address to the "elders," whom the Lord had raised up in its midst—men of age and Christian experience, whom the Holy Ghost had made "overseers" to feed and guide the saints—tells how deeply his heart was exercised on their behalf, and his prophetic warning of evils to arise in their midst, with wolves entering in from without, combining to blight their spiritual freshness, cause the fine gold to become dim, and darken the light that shone from the lampstand, may well have put them on their guard and kept them watchful. The Epistle written to this Church some years later, in which the heavenly calling, hope, and destiny of the Church, with the walk and testimony on earth worthy of such a calling, in which no reproofs are found, and no evils dealt with, shows that the "first love" condition was then still found among them. But the enemy was not far off: he never is where there is a church or even an individual standing for God and for Christ among men. Timothy, who had remained in Ephesus (see 1 Tim. i. 3), after Paul had gone to other fields, had to be reminded of the need of firm and faithful dealing with some who were beginning to teach "a different doctrine," and not long after, he had to be reminded that "all that are in Asia" (2 Tim. ii. 15)—which included the Church at Ephesus—had "turned away" from Paul. Probably thirty years later, this "Second Epistle to the Ephesians," as it has been called, was sent, showing how the Lord viewed it, and giving warning and encouragement to all who had a hearing ear. It is worthy of note that in each of the seven messages, the Lord first commends all that He finds according to His mind, before either reproving the evil or setting the way of rectification before them. This is His way, and it ought to be our example. For even where there is much to condemn, and much that is crooked to be set straight, grace never fails to fix upon some bright spot, something that is of God, and to own it. And in this way the confidence of those whose feet require to be washed, and whose ways require to be corrected, is won, and the ears of at least some gained to hear the Word of the Lord.

The titles by which the Lord introduces Himself to this Church are significant. "He that holdeth the seven stars in His right hand," tells that He is the source of power for all true testimony and ministry. All must come from Him. He walks "in the midst" of the lampstands, to watch over,

THE LORD'S FIRST REPROOF

to trim and feed the lamps. He is acquainted with their state, and gives praise or blame as He sees need. And it is His prerogative alone to "remove" any lampstand from its place if it fails to serve the purpose for which He set it there, as it is to reject by vomiting from His mouth (Chap. iii. 16), what has become utterly abhorrent to Him. No such power has He entrusted to man, it is His alone.

First Love Left. The Lord now speaks direct to the assembly He is addressing, through its representative. "I know thy works, and thy toil and patience (endurance)." "I know"—seven times repeated, assures us of His omniscience, everywhere, always. The varied energies too are well defined, "thy works, thy labour, thine endurance," all true and enduring. They had "also tried"—that is tested, pretenders who had arisen among them (Acts xx. 30), who had claimed apostolic powers, and "found them liars," false—false apostles (2 Cor. xi. 13). All this was continued without being "wearied." All here is commendatory. Yet when looked at alongside the Apostle's commendation of the Church in Thessalonica (1 Thess. i. 1-3), the contrast is apparent. There, the three words are found with the secret springs of their action, "work of *faith*, labour of *love*, patience of *hope*," but this motive power is not mentioned in Rev. ii. 2. Had it declined? Surely it had, for the Lord immediately adds—"But I have against thee"—the word *somewhat* is not in the text, nor was it uttered by the Lord, for the charge is serious and must not be minimized by such a word—"that thou hast left thy first love"—"that thou *did'st leave* thy first love"

(R.V.). The first stage in decline had set in. "First love," that fresh, pure, flow of love to Christ which comes from the heart's enjoyment of His love (1 John iv. 19), to us, the "love of thine espousals" as the prophet speaks (Jer. ii. 2), that is of so great esteem in the eyes of the Lord, and which nothing can make up for the lack of. They had "left" it: the motive and spring of all devotion and service had failed, and the Lord knew it. He does not hide it, but lets His people know the loss He has sustained. For love can never be satisfied with less that love. When love fails, all else loses its value (see 1 Cor. xiii.). The next word turns them back to their first estate, "Remember from *whence* thou art fallen"—not how far, but "from whence." It was from Him they had gone, from His bosom, from His side. They were to "remember" this and "Repent." There was nothing outwardly wrong, nothing that needed reproof in doctrine or rectification in practice, or even reviving in energy. All was going on as men would say, prosperously. But in His estimation they had "fallen," and they needed to "repent." The Lord's standard is high, and it is well to test ourselves by it. "And do the first works," for they too had ceased. Was this a reference to the clean sweep "not a few" of them made at the time of their conversion, when they burned their ungodly books, worth £1,875, in a public bonfire before all (Acts xix. 19)—a true evidence that old things had passed away? With some, at anyrate, of our own time, there is need for a second cleaning out, for some things are apt to quietly return into our lives which were once expunged from them. The next note is solemn: "But if not, I am coming to thee, and will remove thy lampstand out of its place, except thou repent." This does not mean that the saints were to be severed from Christ and perish, or that the Church would cease to be seen in Ephesus, but that it would lose its place of pre-eminence as representing Him there; but just as a Christian may long continue on earth after he has ceased to be a witness for God among men, so may a Church, after it has lost its place as God's corporate witness to His truth in the place where it is.

Nicolaitanism. One evil, hated by the Lord and the saints addressed, is now named, "the deeds of the Nicolaitanes." Who were these? Commentators are puzzled, and all sorts of guesses have been made. That they represent some evil principle is clear. Here their "deeds" are hated in Ephesus, but their "doctrine" is allowed in Pergamos. The word means, "those who conquer the people" —the laity, and claim for themselves the place of "clergy," which means the Lord's lot (see 1 Pet. v. 3), lording it over others, and claiming the sole right of conducting the worship of the saints, all of whom are priests to God (1 Pet. ii. 5). This was the first appearance of clerisy in the church, which as spiritual condition declines, and the love of the many waxes cold, grows apace. For where there is first a leaning on gifted individuals, and a preference for a sermon, rather than to worship God by the Spirit, it is an easy step to next appoint and pay one to do the whole for them. And the supply is usually equal to the demand. For when Israel want a king to take the place that the Lord has hitherto held in their midst (1 Sam. x. 19), some Saul is easily found for the post. The promise to the overcomer to "eat of the tree of life," which was forfeited by Adam's disobedience, secured for all His own by Christ, and "given" by Him to all who hear and heed His words, is a fitting close to this message. Viewed prophetically, the Ephesian condition ended about A.D. 160.

Smyrna. Of the beginning of the Church here, or by whose ministry it was formed, we have no record in Scripture. The city was large and prosperous, it lay some 40 miles north of Ephesus, was in some respects its rival, and almost from the beginning of the Gospel in Asia, its people were persecutors of the Christians. Here Polycarp, the disciple and friend of John, was, it is recorded, slain for his faith about A.D. 168, in his 90th year. In Smyrna, the first great Pagan persecution, which raged throughout Asia, had its chief agents. The word "Smyrna" signifies *Myrrh*—a fragrant spice used for embalming the dead, derived it is said by "bleeding" the plant. The whole wording of the message is aglow with tribulation, persecution, suffering, and death. The Lord presents Himself as the First and the Last, "who became dead and lived again" (R.V.), reminding these suffering saints of His, that through death to life is the appointed path for them as it was to Him, and that to those who are "faithful unto death," there will be "a victor's crown of life." First love having been left, the Lord permits the world, instigated by the devil, as is here revealed (ver. 10), to raise the fierce fires of persecution, to arrest decline, and bring through trials of faith a people purged of their dross. The words, "I know thy tribulation and poverty (but thou art rich)," have been generally taken as wholly full of grace and consolation. But the words, "thou art rich," or "thou hast waxed rich"—read as a parenthesis, may point to worldly advantage gained by unfaithfulness to Christ, which their tribulation would deprive them of,—an experience not uncommon to saints when they gain worldly gear by alliance with the ungodly.

Foes Within. Judaism, all along the enemy of true Christianity (Acts xv. 1), had arisen within, while Pagan persecution raged without. Some calling themselves "Jews," claiming after some manner to be God's chosen, to have preferential claims to be His elect above the general company of the saints, but who are described by the Lord in their true character as a "synagogue of Satan"— a gathering together of a promiscuous crowd—as the word synagogue implies—a rabble instigated by Satan, the *Adversary*, to oppose and imitate the true *ecclesia*, God's outcalling from the world gathered to the Lord's Name. The same form of opposition appears in the Philadelphian Church, near the last, where it opposes devotion to Christ in times of easy *profession*, as here in dire *persecution*.

The Enemy Without. Another malignant foe was soon to use his power against them, "the Devil," the Destroyer and Slanderer, stirring up the heathen rulers to cast some of them "into prison," in order that they might be tested. This gathering storm begun under Nero and Domitian, and it is said continued under *ten* emperors, during a period of over 230 years,* the last under Diocletian, lasting *ten* years, which the period of "ten days" may symbolise. In any case it tells that God had set a limit to Satan's rage, beyond which he could not pass, nor continue his opposition any longer than God's purpose had been served, in arresting the decline of His people, and hindering that affinity with the world toward which they had been advancing. The cases of Job and Peter show the same principle at work in the lives of individual saints. The Devil is permitted by God to chastise and sift, in order to purge the true gold from its dross, and the wheat from its chaff, but he dare not go a step beyond God's permission (Job i. 12). To this suffering Church the assuring word is "Fear not the things which thou art about to suffer"; the Lord would not suffer them to be tried beyond what they could bear (1 Cor. x. 13). He would be with them while passing through the fires (Isa. xliii. 2), and, like the three Hebrew youths in the furnace (Dan. iii. 25), they would lose nothing but their *bonds*. His word of assurance is the promise: "Be thou faithful unto death, and I will give thee a Victor's Crown of Life"—that crown which goes to those who "love Him," more than life (James i. 12), and hold fast to Him and His Word, after the pattern the Perfect Examplar set before them, becoming obedient even "unto death" (Phil. ii. 8). To the "overcomer," the promise is that he shall in nowise be hurt of the "second death." He may be

* Began under Nero, A.D. 54, ended under Diocletian, A.D 284.

thrown to the lions in the Ampitheatre, or kindled as a torch to light up the emperor's gardens, but "the second death," worse by far than any first death man could devise, would not even "hurt," much less devour. For as the three faithful Hebrew witnesses passed through the flame of Babylon's furnace, without the smell of fire on their garments, or a hair of their head singed, while the same fire instantly destroyed the men who cast them into it, so shall all who are of faith triumph in life or in death, and therefore "overcome the world" (1 John v. 4).

Pergamos. This city—not elsewhere named in the New Testament—the capital of Mysia, and a royal residence, was reckoned one of the finest cities of Pro-consular Asia. The Church in it has the distinction that it is addressed by the Lord as "dwelling" in the place "where Satan's throne is" (R.V.), and "where Satan dwelleth." This may refer to the fact that it was the centre of idolatry, which is demon-worship, Divine honours being paid to the emperors there, and that from Pergamos, the seat of government, persecuting edicts were issued against the Christians, and by the devil's rage as a roaring lion, thousands upon thousands were slain. But Pergamos, in another and to the Church more dangerous form, had now become the place of the "throne," and the "dwelling" of Satan. The Union of the Church with the world was to have its completion soon, and this Church was to be the exemplification of it. If Satan's rage cannot exterminate Christianity, what if his craft can corrupt it? If the devil cannot as "a roaring lion" (1 Pet. v. 8) devour, he may as a "subtle serpent" beguile (2 Cor. xi. 3). The close of the persecutions of Diocletian, the last of the ten, was followed by the reign of Constantine, who accepted Christianity as his religion (it is very questionable if he ever accepted Christ and was born again), and giving his patronage to the Church, he succeeded in seducing it from the place of separation into which the call of God had brought it, bringing it into union with the State. This unholy alliance is evidently hinted at in the words "I know *where* thou dwellest"—for these words mean more than mere locality: they express a moral and solemn significance. "*Dwellers* on earth" (Rev. iii. 10: xi. 10), and "who *mind* earthly things" (Phil. iii. 19), are words that mark out a class whose hearts and interests are set on things below, a people who have seen, and it may be "tasted" of heavenly things, but who prefer the earthly instead.

2. The word "Pergamos" or "Pergamum," includes a word which means *marriage*, and the condition here is that of a courtship, followed by a marriage, with the world. Their "friendship" (James iv. 4), had developed into "love" (1 John ii. 16), and here they clasp hands and after the "marriage" dwell together, under the shadow of "Satan's throne," for he is the world's "prince." To this Church the Lord presents Himself as "He that has the sharp two-edged sword" (ver. 12), for to His people in such a condition He must speak sharp and searching words, leading them to self-judgment (Heb. v. 12). Soft and delectable things are not in season

to Christians in worldly alliances; they must have their conscience searched before their hearts can be comforted. God's order is to make His people clean first, and warm next; they must be "purified by obeying the truth," in order to "love with a true heart fervently" (1 Peter i. 22). And yet the Lord, as is His way, recognises what is still found of His grace among them. He says "thou holdest fast My Name, and hast not denied My faith." They had not let go the vitals of their faith, nor as yet discarded the Name of their Lord for another. They had not, however, shared the full brunt of persecution, for one "Antipas" ("one against all,") whom the Lord dignifies with the title "My faithful witness, who was slain among *you*," had stood up for the faith and fallen alone. Was it that they had begun to shirk the Cross, and that this "faithful one" (R.V.), had fallen "among them," not one standing by him? When Christians fraternise with the world, they do not usually have the courage to stand up for what they believe, but will remain silent, even if their faithful brethren are illtreated and martyred by those with whom they go hand in hand.

Balaam's Doctrine. A definite charge of harbouring teachers of evil doctrine is, for the first time, made against the Church. The Lord had this "against" them. He had already challenged evil "deeds," now He exposes the "doctrine" that produces the deeds. For while it is true that one may hold right doctrine intellectually, and yet show little fruit of it in his life, none can live to please God who give up His truth, or who are under the power of error. Truth sanctifies (John xvii. 17), but error corrupts (2 Tim. ii. 17). The exact form of this evil doctrine is named by the Lord. It is the "doctrine of Balaam"—the man who had the Word of the Lord in his mouth (Numb. xxiii. 5), but who "loved the wages of unrighteousness" (2 ii. 15), and sold his service to the heathen king of Moab, first to curse, and when that failed, to corrupt the people of Israel. The sordid story of this money-loving prophet's seduction of Israel's sons, from the place of separation to which God had called them (Exod. xix. 6: Deut. vii. 2-5), into unholy alliance with the daughters of Moab, is told by God in Numbers xxv. 1-8. Nothing is hid. Foiled in his efforts to curse the people whom God had blessed, in whose midst He dwelt (Numb. xxiii. 21), and ruled, this wily prophet instructed the Moabite king how to work out a device to cast a "stumbling-block"—a snare, before the feet of the men of Israel. The women of Moab were used as the bait, and they led their victims to worship their idols. The judgment of God was speedily inflicted on the guilty alliance, and 24,000 of the people fell under the plague at Baal-peor. The reference to this event by the Lord, and the use He makes of it to denounce the guilty union of the Church with the world, is very solemn. Inside this Church of His at Pergamos, there were those who were acting the part of Balaam over again. They were instructing the world to lay baits to seduce the Church, to illicit intercourse with it, and to "join" itself with it. This, in the plain language of the Word is called fornication (ver, 21). As Israel, who was regarded as "married" to Jehovah and His covenant people, were charged with *adultery* when they mingled themselves with the nations, so the Church as a "chaste virgin," who has been "espoused" to Christ (2 Cor. xi. 2), by unholy alliance with the Christ-rejecting world, is regarded by her Lord as guilty of spiritual fornication. And just as the actual sin is the most awful charge that can be laid to any hitherto chaste person, so the admixture religiously of those who "belong to Christ" (Mark ix. 41), with His enemies, is the foulest blot a Church or a Christian can bear in His sight. Yet how common, yea, how popular it is! And how the Balaam prophets of our time glory over the Church unions they make, and the amalgamations they achieve, without a single reference as to what God has said about them (see James iv. 4, R.V.). The Church in Pergamos is not charged with holding or teaching these doctrines, but it had tolerated and not resisted or judged those who did. And in the Lord's estimation, to tolerate evil doctrine is to connive with it (2 John 10, 11). Yet the Lord distinguishes, for in His call to repentance He warns them that if they as a Church fail, He will come to the whole of them "quickly," to deal in some penal manner with them for their unfaithfulness, but He will "fight against *them*"—make war against *them* (R.V.), the actual teachers of the evil doctrine. Thus while all are guilty, all are not equally guilty, and the righteous Lord has compassion, "making a difference" (Jude 22, 23). This should be noted by all who are called upon to judge evil, and deal with those actively or passively connected with it.

The theory that all who are within the same walls with an evil-doer must be equally evil, and so judged, is not the principle of the Book of God. Grace discriminates, while holiness judges evil. Here also the Nicolaitane "deeds" had become "doctrines," for what men "do" they will soon find something in the Bible which they will twist to support their deeds, and give out as "doctrine," authorising them. These two forms of evil often combine; the clerics, being the leaders in all forms of worldliness, and the promoters of worldly practices within the Church. The call to each is to hear "what the Spirit saith to the Churches," for while the message is primarily to Pergamos, it has that in it which all need to hear and heed, which the ever present Spirit, indwelling and ministering to the saints, makes "present truth" to all.

Gifts and Rewards. To the "overcomer" amid such conditions there is the promise of two special gifts and rewards from the Lord. "I will give of the hidden manna," and "I will give a white stone." The manna was Israel's wilderness food (Exod. xvii.): "the hidden manna" (ver. 15), the memorial of God's faithfulness in providing for them all the years of their pilgrimage way, carried into Canaan in the Ark. So shall it be in heaven. We shall see and learn and know all the way the Lord hath led us, and how His mercies were "new to us every morning" (Lam. iii. 23), all the days. The "white stone"—said to be the symbol of acquittal, and of approval in social circles, the receiver having it given him secretly with his name engraved on it— here tells that there will be a personal intimacy between the glorified Lord and His own, as well as a public reward of faithfulness.

The Pergamos period extends from Constantine's day till about A.D. 606. It was during this period that the Church became united to the world, and under the power of clerisy and politics, lost its power for testimony, and sank into utter worldliness. The story of how Constantine became a nominal Christian by means of a dream, how he adopted the Cross as his standard, acknowledged it as the cause of his victory, became Head of the Church while continuing High Priest of the heathen, is well known and generally gloried in as a triumph of Christianity over Paganism. But here we learn the Lord's estimate of it, very different indeed from man's, and it ought to warn all of the danger of unhallowed unions with the world.

Thyatira. To this Church, the Lord presents Himself under a title and in symbols expressing Divine power to search out evil and to judge it. He speaks as "the Son of God who hath His eyes like a flame of fire, and His feet like unto burnished brass." As Son of God He is Life-giver (John v. 25), and to Him alone this honour belongs. To a Church, which is the chosen representative of that vast system in which Mariolatry has obscured the Divine Sonship, by worshipping a babe in the arms of its mother, whom they name "mother of God" is significant. He is the "searcher of hearts" (ver. 23), and what His eyes "as a flame of fire" discover, His "feet" will tread in judgment, just and inflexible. Yet, even here He finds something to commend. He says "I know thy works, and love and faith and service, and thine endurance." In the midst of grave conditions, calling forth solemn denunciation and stern rebuke, He commends what He finds in their midst. "Works" are twice named, "the last more than the first." Here too, "love" and "service," which found their full manifestation in the life of the Lord (John xiii. 1, 2), and are the true expressions of spiritual liberty (Gal. v. 13), are praised, and would be valued by the Lord in those who were godly. But a grave indictment immediately follows, for this Church had gone far beyond anything we have yet heard of, in permitting an evil system to grow up unchecked in its midst. "But I have against thee" (R.V.)—the words "a few things" are not in the original Text, for the Lord does not minimize the evil—"that thou sufferest the woman," or "thy wife"—Jezebel, who "calleth herself a prophetess." Here a woman, and she so wedded to the church as to be no more twain, but one with it, is to the front and in the place of power, not the Man as Lord and Head (Eph.v.23). Jezebel, after whom this vile system is named, was a Zidonian princess, an idolater and a persecutor, who stirred up Ahab, a weak tool in her hands, to lead God's people Israel to worship Baal (1 Kings xvi. 31), and kept around her table four hundred prophets for the carrying out of her diabolical plans. She represents Popery as a system, which claims to be the mouthpiece of God. "Hear the Church" is her cry. The voice of the Church is the voice of God; her teaching is inerrant, her Popes infallible. She is the ruler of nations, and for centuries held them in her grasp. In her teaching she "leads

My servants astray" into unholy alliance with the nations, whose crowns were claimed and worn by men professing to be servants of the meek and lowly Jesus, while the Pope, the Vicar of Jesus Christ on earth, was ruler of emperors and kings. This continued "throughout the dark ages," in which not a vestige of the Gospel remained in the teaching of the Church. "Idolatry" in the worship of Mary, the adoration of "saints," and the veneration of "sacred places" and spiritual fornication—illicit intercourse with the world, were and are Rome's teachings, and her final state as Babylon (Rev. xvii.), shows that this she ever will be until the day of her doom. Time for repentance given has wrought no change; in principle and in practice wherever she dares, Popery is a Jezebel persecutor and murdress still. And the Divine verdict here is "she will *not* repent"—no, never. Verses 22, 23, give three circles, each threatened with judgment by the Lord. 1. Jezebel herself the corrupt system. 2. Those who traffic with her. 3. Her children: systems which have sprung from Popery, received her principles, copied her ways, and are Papacy in everything but the name, who are masquerading as Protestant Churches, while actually in league with Popery: these, the Lord says, unless they "repent of their works"—for subscribing to a creed will not do—He will "kill with death," and their judgment will be a lesson to "all the churches," and will show that the infliction, whatever it may be, is present, not future judgment. Already such judgment has begun at "the house of God" (1 Pet. iv. 17), and there has been enough to cause some searchings of heart, as to whether the Lord is not giving "each according to their works," even here and now.

The Remnant. Amid all the corruption the living Lord, whose searching eyes allow nothing to pass, sees a faithful remnant, who, although not outwardly separate from this corrupt Church, were witnesses against its evil ways, and utterly repudiated its corrupt teaching. To them the word is given, "To you I say—the rest who are in Thyatira who have not this doctrine." In the darkest times of the medieval Church, the Waldenses, Lollards, and others were true witnesses for Christ, simple souls who had not known "the depths of Satan." They were the sufferers and martyrs of the Papal period, and to their time the word Thyatira, which signifies *Bruised Incense*, applies. On them the Lord lays no other burden than to "hold fast" what they had, and await His coming again. And to all such, He gives the promise of "authority over the nations"—not now as Rome seeks, but with Himself when He reigns. And before that time the sweet promise of Himself as "the Morning Star"— the name that He bears in relation to His Church (Rev. xxii. 16), and His coming for His people, which will be the first stage of His progress towards His rule of the world, and His forthshining in His kingdom as the "Sun of Righteousness" (Mal.iv.2).

CHAPTER III.

SYNOPSIS:—SARDIS: Profession without Life—Warning and Promise—Protestantism. PHILADELPHIA: Honouring the Lord, His Name, and Word—Modern Judiasm—The Present Period. LAODICEA: Self-satisfaction—Lukewarm Profession—The Lord Outside—The End of Christendom.

IN this Chapter, other forms of decline in spiritual purity, power, and testimony, are laid to the charge of His Churches by the Lord, who walks among them. But while decline continues and advances, there is revival and return to Himself which the Lord appreciates and commends, holding forth present blessing with future recompense to all who overcome and are true to Him, in the times through which they pass. These three closing messages are of special interest to us of these last times.

Sardis. By common consent, the message to the Church in Thyatira presents the Papal system as the Lord sees it, and here what succeed its—Protestantism. The condition is one of lifeless profession, in which the Lord finds nothing to commend, much to reprove, with a threat that His coming will find them unprepared, ending with a bright promise to "the few," who, in the midst of such conditions, kept their garments undefiled, and a reward to him who overcomes, with his name being confessed before the Father. Sardis, which signifies *The Things that Remain*, represents the condition of Protestantism after the Reformation, and as it exists to-day. This, like Popery, will continue to the end. The title assumed by the Lord here, tells that in His hand is all power for government, and all gifts for ministry, in His Church. In Popery, the Pontiff, the so-called Vicar of Christ, claims to have all power, represented by the "keys" that he bears, and from him in a line of "succession" all ministry is handed on. In Protestantism, kings and landowners hold and bestow benefices, or the people choose their own pastors and rulers. Christ is not owned as the Source and Giver of all His Church needs, for service and testimony, and the result in most cases is an inefficient, formal, and lifeless ministry, for which men qualify and compete as in any other profession. And as is the pulpit so is the pew. The majority of Church members neither require or profess to be born again. A "name to live" while dead, is the Lord's own description of much that bears His Name, and His call is to those who have life and are His, in the midst of such conditions, to "be watchful" and "strengthen the things that remain." There is no charge of false teaching, or of infallibility here, but the good that remains is "ready to die," and the works begun in separating from the corruptions of Popery had not been "found complete" by Christ before His God. They may be boasted in by Protestants, but they are imperfect and lacking before God. The truths recovered by Luther and his co-workers, the Bible put into the hands of the

A FAITHFUL FEW AMID LIFELESS PROFESSION

people, the liberty to worship and serve "as it is written," have not been used as they ought. Therefore the call is to "remember" and "repent," in view of what has been given, and how, holding fast the great truths afresh committed in Reformation times by the energy of the Spirit, not as dead "creeds" and nominal "confessions of faith," but as the Word of God working effectually (1 Thess. ii. 13). Judgment must come upon all who refuse, and it will in the same form as upon the sleeping world in thief-like stealth, when least expected (1 Thess. v. 2, 3).

The Undefiled. As in Thyatira a "remnant" was found who gave joy to the Lord, who kept themselves as separate from the corruptions of their time as they were allowed, so here in Sardis "a few names" are found of His "own sheep," who still heard His voice and followed Him (John x. 27), keeping their garments "undefiled," and themselves unspotted from the world (Jas. i. 27). To them it will be given to walk with the Lord in purity, not in virtue of their lives, for the believer's meetness for a part in the inheritance of the saints in light is found in the blood of Christ shed for his redemption, and the fitness imparted by the Spirit in his regeneration (Col. i. 12). But they had proved it so by their "worthy" walk (Col. i. 10). "White raiment" will tell the Divine appreciation of their path, and their names erased from all records of earthly fame because of their allegiance to Christ, will be read forth from the Book of Life, the register of the true heavenly family, who are to shine as the sun in the Father's Kingdom (Matth. xiii. 43).

The Sardis condition, which may be said to have begun when Protestantism was established as a State Religion, by the Second Diet of Spires, in 1529, continues to the end.

Philadelphia. The Church here has no reproofs and no threatenings from the Lord. There is no outward display, but He has His right place, and His Name and Word are owned and honoured. There is only a "little strength," but it is used in His interests and His service. "*The* synagogue of Satan," which in Smyrna was named, re-appears here, evidently in organised form, a promiscuous gathering up with a patched-up Judaistic ritual, having great pretensions and high claims, but as the Lord reckons, a work and device of "Satan," to imitate and oppose what is the work of the Spirit, in gathering *out* from the world a people *unto* the confession of the Name of the Lord, whose Word they acknowledge as their only guide. Such were the elements in the Philadelphian Church, the name meaning *Brotherly Love*, the true spiritual bond that kept it together. In the *individual* aspect it tells what even a feeble few of the Lord's true disciples, owning His Name and Word, with love abounding among them, may attain even now, while in the *historic* view it surely represents a revival and return to the Lord and His truth among His own, who find themselves together thus before the end. The "remnant" acknowledged "in Thyatira" as resenting the wrong, yet not wholly separate from it, and the "few names" of those who kept their garments undefiled, while yet "in Sardis," are here seen outside in separation from the mass, opposed by "Satan's synagogue," but found together, in feebleness owning the Name and Word of the Lord. There is no remnant addressed here, for the whole company partake of the remnant character, and have got a step further in actual and visible separation, from the religious world—not THE Pentecostal or Apostolic Church reconstructed as at the beginning, nor with any hope of gaining wide influence or great numbers, but with "an open door" given by the Lord and a "little power" to use it, "holding fast" (ver. 11) what it has, while looking for the Lord to come and take them from the scene, "out of the hour" that is about to come to try them, "the dwellers on the earth"—religious worldlings with a name to live "who mind earthly things" (Phil. iii. 19).

The promise to him that overcomes—that holds on His way, and holds fast that which he has from the Lord, humbly but firmly standing steadfast, is that he shall be made "a pillar" in God's temple, an illusion to Solomon's pillars of *stability* and *strength*, Jachin and Boaz (1 Kings vii. 21), never to be moved from that place of honour in which the Lord will place him. Here is encouragement, cheer and promise, indeed, to all who make it their aim to do what pleases Christ, whatever others think and say about them. Enough it is for such to experience in their lowly path of obedience that the Lord loves them (John xiv. 23), and that one day He will cause even their opposers to "know" (ver. 9) it, openly and publicly. The Philadelphian condition may surely be associated with the fresh energy of the Spirit, put forth at various times and through varied instrumentalities during the past and present centuries, in which the Lord has awakened His people to the value of His Word, and enabled many to return to the simplicity of His way, individually in their lives, and collectively in their worship and testimony. This will continue until He comes.

Laodicea. This Church is once named before in the New Testament, by Paul, in Col. iv. 16. Of its origin, growth, and decline, there is no record. But it may be inferred from the fact that the Epistle to the Colossians was to be passed on to that Church, to be read in it, and the Epistle in that Church's possession—believed by many to have been the Epistle to the Ephesians, passed around as a circular letter, both of which contain the highest truths, which only the spiritual were capable of understanding aright—that the Laodicean company was at one time in a good spiritual condition, not unlike the Church at Ephesus before it left its first love. But now, alas! how changed. Lukewarm toward Christ, poor and blind in His judgment, but rich and increased with goods, in need of nothing, in its own. The word means "*The Rights of the People*"—a popular cry of the time, with little consideration of what pleases the Lord.

The Lord asserts His threefold Title here. He is "The Amen," meaning that every word He speaks is guaranteed, every promise He gives fulfilled, so unlike all that men and churches are. "The Beginning of the Creation of God"—God's new creation of which He is Firstborn and Head (Col. i. 15-17), all standing in eternal security "in

"CAUGHT UP" AND "SPUED OUT"

Him" in the power of redemption, never to fall or fail. But this Church had fallen so low in its spiritual condition that the Lord says of it, "Thou art wretched, and miserable, and poor." And so utterly nauseous was its condition to Him, that He uses concerning it the awful words "I am about to spue thee out of My mouth," that is, to utterly reject it as something He can no longer own. This is the end of that which, with lofty pretension, claims to be His Church up to the hour of its excision, which will be marked by the rapture of all His true saints to heaven. The true will be "caught up," the false will be "spued forth."

Lukewarm. The word is generally used as if it meant lacking in fervour and only half-hearted. But this is not its meaning, for the Lord does not reject but always seeks to restore His own from this condition. It is the mixture of hot and cold in one vessel, the world in its ungodliness and religion in one camp; pleasure and piety, the communion table and the theatre attended by the same people, sometimes on the same day. Great swelling words of "Glory to God" with unblushing pride and vanity on the same lip. This the Lord will not own, and He here lets us know it. It was utterly insensible, for the Lord says "Thou *knowest* not." Like Samson, when shorn of His strength, and lying helpless in Delilah's lap, knowing not that the Lord had departed from Him (Judges xvi. 19, 20), so it knew not its state before the Lord. An earnest word of "counsel" to deal direct with Himself, and a gracious word to remind whoever of His own may be there, that whom He "loves" He "chastens," with a call to stir themselves to repentance, closes the general message. Then the last great word—generally used as a Gospel text (ver. 20), but really a call to the saved—from Himself, now outside the door, knocking to awake His own to come *out* unto Him, with the gracious word of promise that He will "come in to him"—not to the Church, and "sup with Him"—assuring the individual who hears and heeds His call, that whatever may be lost by obedience to His Word, He will make up by fellowship with Himself.

The Overcomer here is to be set down with the victorious Lord on His own throne, by His side, in the day of His coming glory, even as He has now "sat down" with His Father on His throne—a position which is heaven's own answer to, and reward of, His perfect obedience here (Phil. ii. 8, 9), in the face of the world's verdict in giving Him a felon's cross. And that silent, unchallenged leading up to the place of highest honour in heaven, and seating of the earth-rejected Son of God on the right hand of the Majesty on high, augurs what awaits those who will shortly be brought up to sit with Christ on His throne, and tells the way by which they will come.

Thus ends "the things that are," as the Lord sees and describes them. No more are Churches seen or addressed on earth: no longer do lampstands hold up lights of bright or fading testimony in the world. With Chapter iii. the present Church-age ends, and with Chapter iv. "the things which shall be after these" begin.

CHAPTER IV.

SYNOPSIS:—A Door opened in Heaven—John caught up—The Throne and the Throne-Sitter—The Crowned Elders and their Place—The Living Creatures and their Worship.

THE opening words of this Chapter, "after these things," begin the third division and the main theme of the Book. John had been called to see in symbol, and to hear from the living Lord, through His angel, the record of His judgment on the testimony of His Church on earth, and now "after these things" had fulfilled their course, he "looked" for what was to follow. Lamps were no longer to be seen giving heaven's light on earth. But the eyes of the Seer turning toward heaven meet a new vision. "Behold a door opened in heaven." Heaven had been opened before on great occasions. Once to testify that the Beloved Son was on earth (Matth. iii. 17); once to show a martyred saint that He had gone back to the right hand of God, and was ready to receive him there (Acts vii. 56), and once to show by the symbolic sheet, let down from and taken up again to heaven, the fitness of God's called out and cleansed heavenly people, for the home to which they are destined (Acts x. 11-16). Here is "a door opened," with a trumpet-like Voice of a heavenly Speaker, the same as he had heard in Chap i. 11, but now in a new position, speaking to a man on earth, in words which his trained ear understood, followed by his being lifted from the earth upon which he stood into that heaven, to be shown "the things which must come to pass after these," things not one of which can take place while the present age of the presence of the Church on earth continues, but which as we here learn will begin immediately it has been removed. It has been asked by some, Where in this Book of Revelation do we see the removal of the saints from earth to heaven? The answer is,—*here*, stated in the language of sign and symbol, in common with the rest of the teaching of this Book. John, who here is their representative, is called to "Come up hither," and immediately he is "in the Spirit" and in presence of "a throne set in heaven."

The Lord's word concerning John, spoken on the Lake shore, misinterpreted by his fellow-disciples, but evidently well understood by him, "If I will that he tarry till I come" (John xxi. 21-23), has here its fulfilment and its interpretation. For John in this symbolic chapter appears as the foreshadowing figure of the saints who will be "caught up" into heaven, when the Lord comes to the air, with personal "shout" and "Archangel's Voice" and "trump of God," and like Enoch, of antedeluvian times, they will not be "found" on earth when judgments from the throne begin to descend upon it. From this point onward, through all the changing scenes of this Book of judgment, we hear no more of churches on earth, or of saints of the

Church, the body of Christ, as distinct from Jew and Gentile, with heavenly hopes for which they wait. There will be saints and sufferers, witnesses and martyrs, passing through, enduring and coming out from "the great tribulation," to find their destined places in heavenly courts "before the throne" (Chap. vii. 13-16), but the saints of past and present dispensations are not found on earth during these scenes, for they will be removed from it before the Apocalyptic judgments begin.

The Throne of God. The sight which first meets the Seer in the heavenly scene upon which he now enters, is "a throne set"—firmly established in the heavens, stable and fast, which no rising rebellion in the earth below can reach, and no opposition from men, even though their rulers "set themselves" (Psa. ii. 2) and unite to defy God, can shake. Far above all the surging, seething mass, "the Lord's throne is in heaven" (Psa. xi. 4). And on the throne a Sitter is seen: "One who sat, like in appearance to a jasper and a sardius stone," God dwelling in light whom no man can approach, and whose essential glory no man hath seen or can see (1 Tim. vi. 16). Yet by means of symbols, which we may in measure apprehend, He is here declared as in redemption He is known. The jasper and sardius were the first and last of the twelve precious stones on Aaron's breastplate (Exod. xxviii. 17-20), the former transparent and brilliant, "clear as crystal" (Chap. xxi. 11), by some believed to be what we know as the diamond, which, in Chap. xxi. 11, symbolises the light and glory of God. The sardius or sardine, blood colour, expresses His grace in atonement, and His justice in retribution. "A rainbow round the throne"—not a part as now we see it—is the witness to God's covenant with Noah regarding the earth (Gen. ix. 9-17), which will be remembered even in time of judgment (Chap. x. 1), for that judgment is "to destroy those that destroy the earth" (Chap. xi. 18).

The Crowned Elders. Seated on twenty-four thrones, placed around the central Throne, John sees twenty-four elders clothed in white and crowned with crowns of gold. Who are these? They are redeemed and glorified saints in resurrection bodies. Their number twenty-four, is a reference to the twenty-four courses into which David divided the priesthood, in view of the worship to be established in the temple, to be built by Solomon his son, a type of Christ in resurrection glory. These served in turn throughout the sacred year (Luke i. 5-9). Here we see represented the whole of the heavenly, "holy" (1 Pet. ii. 5), and "royal priesthood," who had succeeded each other on earth throughout the entire period of the Great High Priest's session at God's right hand in heaven (Heb. viii. 1: x. 12), and the Comforter's presence with them here on earth.* Their white garments tell of their unsullied purity, their meetness (Col. i. 12) for the sphere they occupy as priests unto God. "Crowns of gold" bespeak their dignity as kings. The former symbolise the glorified saints as

---

*Some think that these crowned elders represent the saints of former ages, while the living ones of ver. 6 symbolise "the Church of the First-born." That both will share in the first Resurrection we know from 1 Cor. xv. 23.

THE GLORIFIED SAINTS

worshippers Godward, the latter as rulers manward, for they are both, as is sung of them in Chap. v. 10, "Thou hast made them to God *kings* and *priests*, and they shall reign." These are the redeemed, all at last brought home, and here seated and crowned in the presence of God on His throne, not prospectively, nor as disembodied spirits, but in glorified bodies, made like unto their Lord, for they have now seen Him "as He is" (1 John iii. 2). And here it may be remarked that this is not their first appearance in heaven, for at their ascension to meet the Lord in the air, when He receives them to Himself (John xiv. 1-3), He will conduct them to the Father's House, where they are welcomed as children. This is a family scene, the first of the many circles of love and glory into which the Lord will conduct His own. But it is not in keeping with the character of the Book to record scenes in the family character of the saints with the *Father*. The view here is of the same glorified company in their priestly and royal dignity, in presence of the throne of *God*, as Creator and Almighty, in anticipation of the kingdom about to be established through judgment. The throne of God is here seen preparing itself for judgment (Psa. ix. 7), and already out of the throne, go forth "lightnings and voices and thunders," for when the age of grace, "the acceptable year of the Lord," runs out, "the day of vengeance of our God" (Isa. lxii. 1, 2) follows quickly. "Seven lamps of fire burning before the throne." Seven lampstands on earth, upholding lamps, sustained in their testimony by the Spirit indwelling, have been removed, grace has ceased to reign, and here the Spirit is seen in the fulness of His power and sovereignty ready to act in government.

"Before the throne a sea of glass like crystal," takes us back to tabernacle and temple times, in which "patterns of things in the heavens" were seen. Here the allusion is to the Brazen Laver, that stood in the tabernacle court between the altar and the door (Exod. xxx. 21), and to the Brazen Sea in front of Solomon's temple (1 Kings vii. 23-37), at which the priesthood daily cleansed themselves for worship and service. But here in the presence of the throne of God the priesthood are seen in perpetual cleanness, with no need of a daily purification, and this "sea like crystal" reflects their beauty, as "clean every whit" and "without spot or wrinkle," in virtue of the work of their great Redeemer. Wilderness sands no more defile their feet: spots contracted from the scenes through which they pass no longer stain their robes! They are now in the light of God.

"Where no shade or stain can enter, or the gold be dim,
In that holiness unsullied, now they gaze on Him."

Living Ones. "In the *midst* of the throne and round about" it, four beasts (living creatures, R.V., literally living ones), are next seen. They are "full of eyes before and behind," knowing intelligently all the past and seeing into the future, instinct in all parts with spiritual life. The first like a Lion, king of beasts, majestic and strong to rule: the second like a Calf or Ox, ready and patient to serve: the third has the face of a Man, sympathetic and intelligent: the fourth like a flying Eagle, with piercing eyes and unwearying wing. Each has six wings, expressing Divine activity in all that concerns the throne around which they wait as attendants. For these "living ones" are the agents employed by God, to execute His purposes and perform His will in all spheres of His government. Once they were angelic, connected with the execution of His *Judgment* on man's sin, accompanying the flaming sword at Eden's gate (Gen. iii. 24), next they are seen on the Mercy-seat above the ark (Exod. xxv. 18), gazing on the Propitiatory, the witness of God's *Grace;* then in the Temple (1 Kings vi. 23-37), looking outward toward *Glory.* A fuller detail of them appears in Ezek. i. 6, where, accompanied by "wheels," they appear beneath the throne, directing the course of God's *Government* in connection with the departure of His manifested presence from the midst of Israel, because of their sin (Exod. x. 1-4). Their position here "in the midst of the throne" identifies them with "the Lamb," who, in Chap. v. 6, is seen there, and points to their close and eternal oneness with Him. For "as the cherubim of glory" in Exod. xxv. were beat out of the same piece of gold as the Propitiatory on which they stood, so these are "all of one" (Heb. ii. 11), and symbolise "the Church of the First-born" in union with Christ, once in grace, now in glory, in unceasing worship and service (ver. 8). They lead in the ascription of thanks to God as Creator, followed by the elders who cast their crowns before the throne, owning their allegiance, and confessing that all they are and have is derived from, and dependent on, the One who sits on that throne.

CHAPTER V.

SYNOPSIS:—The Throne-Sitter and the Book—The Challenge to all Creation—The Lion of Judah—The Once-Slain Lamb takes the Book—The Title Deeds of the Inheritance—The Worthiness of the Lamb Acclaimed—The New Song and the Universal Chorus.

THE throne of God, with Himself seated as sovereign Ruler of the universe alone thereon, is the opening scene of our Chapter. It has undergone a change since the vision of Chapter iv. No longer in the centre, but with crowned elders and cherubim, it now forms part of a circle, into the midst of which at the appointed hour One passes, upon whom all eyes are fixed, bearing the Name of the Lamb. Here also is seen a Book or Roll, written within and without, sealed with seven seals, lying on the outstretched hand of the Throne-Sitter, and a strong angel is heard in a loud voice proclaiming, so as to be heard throughout the whole universe—" Who is worthy to open the Book, and to loose the seals thereof"? (ver. 2). This was the angel's challenge, and there is time given to answer it. The Book contains the full record of the Divine purpose, His determinate counsels concerning the world, and the manner in which they are to be fulfilled. Nothing is left to chance: all is fixed and sure, and the word that has gone forth is "My counsel shall stand, and I will do all My pleasure" (Isa. xlvi. 10). And this counsel of the Most High includes the bringing into subjection to His chosen Ruler of that inheritance, whose sceptre had fallen from the hand of the first Man, who by sin lost the world's sovereignty which had been placed in his hand (Gen. i. 26); since then it has been in the power of the usurper, who claims to it, and to have the right to give it to whomsoever he will (Luke iv. 6). But "power belongeth to God," and since men in all ages and under all conditions have misused the delegated authority committed to their trust, God now holds it in His own hand until one is found who will use it only for God's glory and man's blessing. But where can such a ruler be found? Not one is found to answer the challenge, for whatever men may think of their virtues here, there is not a created being in the universe of God, angelic or human, who lays claim to the right to receive that book from the outstretched hand of God Most High. John "wept much" at the sight. His Lord had wept on earth over Jerusalem's blindness in refusing her Messiah-King, here John weeps in heaven because none can claim the fitness to be the executor of God's purposes of mercy, to Israel and the world, and to redeem by power that inheritance, that purchased possession, which had already been redeemed by price. An elder, one of the glorified beings, whom we have seen seated as crowned priests before God, who are in possession of His mind, now knowing as they are known (1 Cor. xiii. 12), calms and instructs him of One who had "prevailed," had so overcome as to open the seven-sealed book, and by breaking its seals in judgment to clear the earth of all God's foes, and claim it for Him to be ordered and ruled according to His will. And this victorious One is named: He is "the Lion of the Tribe of Judah, the Root of David," dimly foreseen and prophecied of by the dying patriarch Jacob (Gen. xlix. 9), not only David's Son and Heir, but his Root and Lord as well, the One in whom the promises to the earthly people are secured, and by Whom they shall be fulfilled (Psa. lxxii. 17-19).

The Lamb. In response to the call of the elder to "Behold," John raises his eyes to the throne, when lo! a new sight fills his vision. Into the midst of the circle there had come "a Lamb," bearing in His person the evidences that He had come by way of the altar of sacrifice, had been dead and become alive in resurrection. There He is, the Object upon which all eyes are fixed. And this once-slain Lamb, by whose blood the inheritance has been purchased, giving Him the title to it, is the Lion of Judah—a title here only once applied to the Lord—by whose power it is to come into God's possession. The Lamb—or as the word here and elsewhere throughout this Book is, the "little Lamb"*—the One who had been despised and rejected by men on earth, is now exalted to the throne, and about to be invested with all power. "As having been slain": incarnation, redemption, resurrection, all having their part in Him, and leaving their impress on all that He

---

* The usual word for Lamb is *Amnos*, as in John i. 29, 36: 1 Pet. i. 19, but here the diminutive *Arnos*—a young or little Lamb —is used

does. For not only will the memorials of the Cross abide in heaven, but its results will be owned and felt throughout eternity. "Standing" in the midst, for He is no longer seated on the Father's throne (Rev. iii. 21), at the right hand of the Majesty in the heavens (Heb. viii. 1), where in patient grace He has waited for long, but has "risen up" to assume another work to which He has been appointed, and for which He is fully qualified—to rid the world of its usurpers, to put down all false authority, to rule it for God, and finally to deliver up a kingdom worthy of God into His hand at last (1 Cor. xv. 27, 28).

He Takes the Book. Advancing toward the Throne, the Lamb takes the Book from the outstretched right hand of Him who sits on the throne, acknowledging Him as the *Source* of all authority. And the Omnipotent God, in yielding it to the Lamb, owns Him as His acknowledged *Administrator* of that power, the only One to whom He can intrust it with the certainty that it will be used aright. For the Lamb, by His perfect obedience, has proved Himself worthy to be invested with "all authority in heaven and on earth." Thus it is that the Son of Man, as the ancient prophet saw, receives "the dominion from the Ancient of days" (Dan. vii. 13, 14), and as the Nobleman who has gone into a far country receives his kingdom (Luke xix. 12). The power that men of the world have sought but never found, that nations have wared and shed seas of blood to gain, here passes in perfect calm in presence of the whole heavenly host, without one dissenting voice, into the hand of the once-lowly

Nazarene, who had refused it from the hand of Satan (Matth. iv. 9), and recoiled from its offer at the desire of an excited populace (John vi. 15). The symbolic description given of the Lamb in ver. 6, as having "seven horns and seven eyes, which are the seven Spirits of God sent into all the earth," denotes the perfection of His power and knowledge, for all is naked and open to His sight, and what He sees has to be done He has power to effect, in connection with the final adjustment of the universe as His kingdom.

The New Song. As the Book passes into the hand of the Lamb, a thrill passes through the heavenly throng, and extends outward and onward through the entire creation. The living ones and the crowned elders nearest to the throne rise, and, falling prostrate before the Lamb, praise Him. With what rapture does the song of these redeemed and glorified beings arise, as they gaze on Him of whom in earthly years they loved to sing as "the Lamb upon Calvary!" Now they see Him as He is, and know in full measure all that He has done for them, and they sing as never they did or could before, and they all sing, and *each* with a harp of Divine workmanship, suited to the hand that uses it. For each in that great that glorified throng, has his own peculiar part to play, intensely individual though perfectly fitted to the whole in the new song here first sung by the new inhabitants of these heavens which have long been preparing for their coming. And not only have they harps, but "golden bowls full of incense which are the prayers of saints." For these glorified saints

THE SONG OF REDEMPTION

are priests, not to plead or to offer their prayers as if they were mediators or intercessors. Christ alone as the Angel-Priest (Chap. viii. 3, 4), does this, adding the savour of His Name to the prayers of His own, for these simply "have" these bowls in which "the prayers of saints," like the incense of temple times, are stored. And what saints are they whose prayers are so held in remembrance by this heavenly priesthood before the throne of God? Saints of this present time, and of the heavenly calling they cannot be, for these at this time are all in heaven, and they praise but never pray up there. But there will be a feeble company of witnessing and suffering saints, both Jews and Gentiles, who in the midst of awful opposition, persecution, and death, will stand true to God as they know Him, calling for vengeance on their foes, and praying for deliverance for themselves, and these prayers ascend to heaven. The song is a *new* song, not of creation but of redemption accomplished—the praise of the suffering but victorious Lamb of God. And it is not only *of*, but *to* the Lamb. "*Thou* art worthy." Angels are not said to sing: they *say*, "Worthy is the Lamb," speaking *of* Him, but these redeemed ones sing to Him with great intimacy. The A.V. gives "Thou hast redeemed *us* to God by Thy blood, and made *us* kings and priests, and *we* shall reign," but the R.V. has it "Thou wast slain, and didst purchase unto God with Thy blood *men* of every tribe and nation, and madest *them* unto our God a kingdom and priests, and *they* shall reign," which makes the difference that the glorified here sing, not of their own redemption, but of a people on earth for whom they appear, a people who are to reign *on* earth while they reign *over* it. But whichever rendering is adopted—and there is about equal authority for both—the new song is of a redemption standing in the worth of the Lamb which cannot be annulled. And this song first raised by the glorified saints, is caught *up* by myriads of angels, and in an ever-flowing tide swells and rolls on, until every creature in heaven, on earth and under it take their part—the whole vast universe joining in the ascription of praise to God on the throne and unto the Lamb.

In ages past, Divine manifestations were in angelic form, as we learn from Gen. xxii. 11: Exod. xxiii. 20: Jud. vi. 11, but since "the Word became flesh" (John i. 14), passing down lower than angels, to take the bondservant's form (Phil. ii. 7), and having become obedient to death has been exalted as Man, far above angels (1 Pet. iii. 22), His own of this age called out from that world which has rejected Him, are one with Him up there. And not to angels but to redeemed and glorified saints, will the government of the coming age be given (Heb. ii. 5). These are "His fellows" (Heb. i. 9), who suffer with Him here and are to reign with Him there (2 Tim. ii. 12). Angels fall back in Chap. v. into an outer circle to make way for these new administrators who have come to be "in the midst" of the throne as co-heirs with Christ.

CHAPTER VI.

SYNOPSIS:—The Prophetic Period—Its Character and End—An Outline of Events—A Threefold Series of Judgments: Seals, Trumpets, and Vials—The Opening of the Seals and the Results on Earth.

WE now enter on that part of the Revelation which is strictly prophetic, dealing with events on earth. It is of great importance to all who would have a right understanding thereof to keep in mind that during the whole of the period recorded from Chap. vi. to Chap. xix., the saints of the heavenly calling, already glorified in the heavens, are not found amid these judgments which come upon the earth at all. From the time that a door was opened (Chap. iv. 1), to let John *in*—and He is here the representative of the heavenly company—to the opening of heaven to let the Lord with all His saints *out* when they return to the world for judgment (Chap. xix. 11), the saints of the heavenly calling remain, where we last viewed them, with the Lamb, as worshippers and attendants on the throne. The whole of the period of their presence there is characterised by judgment on this earth, which, since the salt has gone from it, has become very corrupt, and since the lights of heaven have gone out, has become dark indeed. We shall see in these Chapters the rise and fall of many gigantic forms of evil, the ascent and downfall of many and varied systems of open hostility to God and His Christ, with the sudden arrest and condign punishment of great and mighty men, who will yet lead millions of mankind in open revolt against the throne in the heavens. In Chap. iv. we have seen that throne prepared for judgment. In the opening of the Seals these judgments begin to come upon men here on earth, in their appointed order, increasing in severity as sinners become more hardened and daring in their opposition to all that bears God's Name. And now that the time of God's patience is past, and the reign of His grace over, judgment returns to righteousness, and sinners get their due reward. The events which these Chapters reveal in symbolic language, are not to be sought for in things that have occurred in the world during the past 1800 years, as many expositors* have attempted to show, with an utter disregard of the key given us by the Lord Himself, at the opening of the Book (Chap. i. 9), in stating its threefold division, which places all that is found from this Chapter to Chapter xix. among "the things that shall be after these," that is after the present dispensation has reached its close.

The history of earth and of the earthly people begins in Chap. vi., and continues till Chap. xix., with several breaks or parenthetic Chapters, notably Chap. vii., which comes in between the sixth and seventh Seals containing God's own record of the sealing of His earthly people. And the whole

*Note A.

chronological events of the Seals, Trumpets, and Vials occur after the heavenly people have gone from earth, and before their return with Christ to it. The *Seals* are opened by the Lamb, the *Trumpets* are sounded by angels, the *Vials* are emptied by God and contain His wrath.

In keeping with our purpose to set forth the main outlines of this prophetic portion of the Book, as simply and plainly as possible, and to seek to learn its practical lessons, we will not go into all minute details, nor dogmatise on points about which we do not consider it is possible at present to speak with authority. There may be much that we have no need to be informed of, that will be made clear to those who will stand amid these awful scenes, and have to act for God therein, which is wisely left in obscurity to us of the present time.

The Seals Opened. At the opening of each of the first four seals, a call from each of the four Cherubs or living ones, brings into view in succession four agencies, in the form of riders upon horses of varied colours. These war-horses with their riders represent defiance of God, which the loud calls from these executors of His judgments bring into visible activity. It was there before, ready to burst forth as a flame, only awaiting some excuse which in the Providence of God is allowed. For in these earlier judgments the means used are less miraculous than later, when men's hearts become so hardened that ordinary measures fail to move them. The heartless crowd in Christendom left on earth, when the Lord calls up His own to heaven, will advance in their godlessness, and the deceiver, under whose power they long had been blinded (2 Cor. iv. 4), will have as his accomplice a new form of delusion (2 Thess. ii. 11), judicially allowed or sent by God upon those who had wilfully refused the Gospel of His salvation. These, with unbelieving Israel and the hordes of heathendom, will compose the populace of earth at this time.

The *First* Seal opened brings forth a white horse with a warrior rider, a conqueror, to whom a victor's crown is given. Some have thought that this first horse, with its rider, represents Christ in His conquests, seeing that He will appear seated on a white horse as in Chap. xix. 11. But this horse and its rider come not from heaven: he only mimics Christ and is of Antichristian origin, a conqueror whose conquests are gained not so much by bloodshed, as by the personal skill he exercises in bringing men into subjection to his rule, as expressed in the "bow" he carries. Thus he gains imperial authority, and extends his empire quickly.

The *Second* Seal having been opened by the Lamb, and the summons "Come," uttered by the second living one—represented by an ox—a fiery red war horse appears, whose rider, bearing a great sword, has authority to "take peace from the earth"—which had evidently succeeded the conquests of the first horseman, who may have introduced a Universal Peace to aid him in his imperial rule. But here the angry passions of men are aroused, possibly by some civil or party strife, and spread unchecked, until "peace" is taken "from the earth," and carnage beyond description world-wide. There is bloodshed enough now, but this will excel, for the restraining hand of God will be withheld, the prayers of groups of godly intercessors will have ceased, the devil will have his way, and the world will learn to its cost what it has chosen, in taking the devil's side against God and Christ.

The *Third* Seal opened brings at the call of the Man-like cherub, a *Black* horse, with a rider holding a pair of balances in his hand, while a voice from the throne proclaims a famine, following civil war, which will especially affect the working classes, whose daily wage of a *denaris* (Matth.xx.2), will only provide the necessary food for the labourer himself. "Oil and Wine" remain unhurt for healing and strength. Thus the Socialists and Labour-leaders, whose gospel of equality for all is now so loudly heard, may learn how heaven regards their movement and where it will end.

The *Fourth* Seal opened brings a *Pale* horse—of an unearthly green-yellow colour, with *Death* as its horseman, followed by a consort and companion named *Hades*. To this rider it was given to slay with sword, with hunger, with death, and by wild beasts—who will again spread themselves over deserted and thinly populated parts of the earth. Death affects man in mortal life. Hades receives the souls of those whom Death cuts off, and holds them in its custody (2 Pet. ii. 9), until the final resurrection for judgment (Rev. xx. 14). Here the ungodly alone are in view. So great will be the influx of lost souls to these dark regions of Hades at this time, that the prophet says "Hades (Sheol, R.V.)

hath enlarged herself, and opened her mouth without measure" (Isa. v. 14). Thus God's "four sore judgments—sword and famine, and noisome beast and pestilence," come upon "a fourth part" of the Roman earth. These come during the first half of Daniel's seventieth week, and are evidently what the Lord referred to in Matth. xxiv. 6-8.

The *Fifth* Seal opened—and there is no Cherub's call following it—John sees "underneath the altar the souls of a company of martyrs who had been "slain for the Word of God and for the testimony which they held." The language is symbolic, the facts are literal. Who are these martyrs and whence came they? That they are not Christians of the present age is certain. They belong to "the things which shall be after these." Their prayer is for vengeance on their foes alive on earth: it is to God as "Sovereign Lord." Such prayer is not in keeping with an age of grace. The Lord's prayer for His crucifiers was, "Father forgive them," and His first martyr Stephen said, "Lord, lay not this sin to their charge." But in the age that follows the present, in which judgment comes openly from heaven on evil doers, such prayers will be in keeping with the time. In many of the Psalms such prayers are found (see Psa. xciv. 1-3: cix. 20), which no intelligent Christian can use as the expression of his desire now. But with an earthly people knowing God as Creator and Judge, it will be different. And such these martyrs are. After the removal of the saints from earth, a work of God's Spirit will begin among the Jewish people, some of whom will go forth preaching the Gospel of the kingdom (Matth.

xxv. 31-46). Their "testimony" will evoke the anger of the ungodly, and they will turn on them and slay them, as the Lord foretells in Matth. xxiv. 9. They are here seen "underneath the altar" (Chap. viii. 5), the place of sacrificial blood (Lev. iv. 7). Their cry is "How long." They are told that their number is yet incomplete, others will yet be slain, and their final glory is not yet. It will come, as Rev. xx. 4 tells us. Meanwhile they each receive a token of God's approval in "a white robe," with the word that assures them that they will "rest a little while"—words that in another connection (Heb. x. 37), are well known to warring saints on earth, and to waiting spirits in heaven.

The *Sixth* Seal opened brings such a convulsion that men not yet quite hardened in heart imagine that the day of wrath, which some of them had heard of in their church-going years, had actually come. And now they pray, and earnestly too, rich men, military leaders, and slaves, all in common, not to God, but to mountains and rocks to hide them from "the wrath of the Lamb," for full well they know in their consciences it must come, whatever they may say with their lips against it. Great convulsions of nature and a complete break up of organized order, with the overturning of Governments, are all implied in the symbolic language in which this cataclysm is described. What a world it will be then! How it will mock all the schemes of world-menders, social reformers, and uplifters of humanity, apart from God and Christ and new birth by the Spirit!

CHAPTER VII.

SYNOPSIS:—Two Parenthetic Scenes—Judgment Restrained—A Jewish Company Sealed for Preservation—A Gentile Multitude: their Place, their Service, their Shepherd, and their share in Millennial Blessing.

FOR a moment the sequence of the history is broken, the succession of the judgments is stayed, and between the opening of the sixth and seventh seals, a lovely picture of God's watchful care over a number of His ancient covenant people Israel, still "beloved for the fathers' sakes" (Rom. xi. 28), who are sealed for preservation amid the coming tribulation, in which they are to be faithful witnesses for God in the midst of unparalleled trial and suffering. This is the first vision. And it is followed by a second, in which a vast unnumbered multitude of Gentiles, out of all nations, are seen, who come out of the Great Tribulation, to stand before the throne of God, and share millennial blessing *under* Christ and his co-heirs who are in heaven. To this intensely interesting parenthesis, this picture of God's mercy in the midst of judgment, it is pleasing to turn, and to remember anew that in His wrath God remembers mercy (Hab. iii. 2), and is ever mindful of His covenant with His own (Psa. cxi. 5). Before the tribulation sets

THE SEALED COMPANY OF JEWISH WITNESSES 89

in God here secures His own, and knows their number, so that not one of them will perish, for their names are in the Book of the Life of the Lamb slain, inscribed there *from* the foundation of the world, as the heavenly people were before the world began (Eph. i. 4: 2 Tim. i. 9).

Judgments Held Back. Four angels, standing on the earth as on a vast plain, are seen restraining the winds, holding in check certain powers of evil struggling to free themselves to hurt those who are here described as "bondservants of our God" (ver. 3). These, an angel bearing the seal of the living God, goes forth to seal upon their foreheads, marking them out as God's possession for His service. This seal is on their foreheads where others may see it, for theirs is no secret discipleship. In these awful times there will be no neutrals, all will bear either the mark of the Beast (Chap. xiii. 6), or the seal of God.

144,000. This number is fixed, its symbolic character signifying *Completeness and Earthly Government*. For these 12,000, from each of the twelve tribes, are to be the nucleus of the new Israel nation who are to be His witness on earth, through which blessing is to reach the world (Psa. lxvii. 1, 2). These witnesses will go forth among "all nations" (Mark xiii. 10), bearing the Gospel of the Kingdom, sowing precious seed, while a later vision of this chapter shows the sheaves they bring back with them rejoicing (Psa. cxxvi. 6).

The Twelve Tribes. As Jacob had thirteen sons, one has to be omitted. In wilderness days this was Levi, whose numbering was taken separately, and who had no inheritance in the land (Numb. i. 47-50). Here, Dan and Ephraim are unnamed. Is it because they were the first to apostatize and harbour idolatry in their midst (Judg. xvii.-xviii.) that God here blots out their names as He threatened? (Deut. xxix. 20-21). Yet at last grace seems to be victorious, for in the millennial distribution of the land among the tribes, they have their places.

A Great Multitude. A second vision given to John in this lull between the sixth and seventh seals is of a great multitude "out of every nation," closely connected with, yet distinct from, the numbered 144,000 of Israel. These are Gentiles, the result of a great work of grace carried on among the nations—probably exclusively among those who had not heard the Gospel during the present age—but who hear from the lips of Jewish missionaries going forth into such lands (Isa. lxvi. 19) the Gospel of the Kingdom (Matth. xxiv. 14). They are not *in* or *of* the Church—the body of Christ, for it has been completed and glorified before they appear. They "*stand* before the throne," not like the crowned elders, who sit on thrones: they wear "white robes" which symbolise purity, they bear palms which express victory, and they cry "Salvation to our God," to which the heavenly host of angels respond—"Amen."

The Elder's Question. To this great sight John is directed by one of the crowned elders, who asks then answers two questions—"Who are they"? and "Whence came they"? giving John and us the very knowledge concerning them we desire. They

THE GENTILE COMPANY BEFORE THE THRONE 91

"come out of the great tribulation" (R.V.)—which is yet future, and will take place after Antichrist has been revealed, in the second half of Daniel's seventieth week. They serve God "day and night in the temple"—which further marks them as an earthly people—for in heaven "no temple" (chap. xxi. 22) is seen, but on earth there will be at this time a rebuilt temple (Ezek. xl.-xliii.) in which Jews and Gentiles (Zech. xiv. 17) will worship and keep the feasts of Jehovah together. "He that sits upon the throne" spreads "His tabernacle over them," and Isa. iv. 56, explains how, giving them shelter, shade, and light. The Lamb on the throne will shepherd and lead them, and they by Him shall be led to "living fountains." And in the exquisite closing words of our chapter, "God Himself" wipes every tear from their eyes, for the days of their sorrow are over, and they have come to the rest, the peace, and the blessedness foreseen by the great prophet of Israel, who spake of their bliss as "the days of heaven upon earth" (Deut. xi. 21).

CHAPTER VIII.

SYNOPSIS:—The Seventh Seal Opened—The Silence in Heaven and its Results on Earth—The Trumpets: their Message and its Meaning—The Angel-Priest at the Two Altars—The Trumpet-Angels and their Place—The Judgment-Angels and their Work—The First Four Trumpets Sound.

THE seventh and last of the Seals on the Roll, received by the Lamb from God Omnipotent on the throne, is now opened—thus completely opening the Sealed Roll and making its contents accessible—and the result is described in the words, "there was silence in heaven for the space of half an hour" (ver. 1). The opening of the former seals had been preparatory, this is the climax as it is the completion. No fresh event is recorded on earth, but a new action is seen preparing in heaven, and a view of what is transpiring there is given—one of these brief parenthetical glimpses so often given in this Book, which show how closely allied events transpiring on earth are with actions prepared in heaven. The hush that falls on heaven for "half-an-hour" does not suggest any pause in the worship of the glorified saints above, but rather to give opportunity for the earthly people, mostly if not wholly Jewish, who have been awakened and converted, and are witnessing on

THE ANGEL-PRIEST AT THE ALTAR 93

earth, to pray. This is the cause of a brief interval in the judgments being sent forth upon the earth. And this solemn pause is used as we learn from verses 3 and 4, to allow the prayers of saints on earth to reach the throne of God, incensed by the hand of the Angel-Priest, who is Christ. For He and no other who could use the efficacy of His own Name and in His own right stand between the throne of God and praying men on earth as "mediator" (1 Tim. ii. 5). To His own in heaven He appears as the Lamb in the midst of the throne, but here in a less known or intimate aspect, as an Angel. The saints for whom He intercedes are not disembodied spirits, as in Chap. vi. 9; no such service is needed for the dead: but the living who are suffering, struggling, and seeking to hold fast some feeble testimony for God on earth—until they are slain, as Chap. vi. 11 tells they shall be—need and have the aid of this Covenant Angel of the earthly Israel of God. The prayers of these saints are for judgment on their foes, and their answer is seen in the symbol of fire from the brazen altar "cast on the earth," with accompanying "voices, and thunders, and lightnings, and an earthquake" (ver. 5). For as sinners become more hardened, God's judgments increase in severity and intensity. We can only glance at these, and mark their course. The language used is symbolic.

The *First* Trumpet brings plagues, like unto those that came upon Egypt, in the day that Pharaoh withstood God's representatives in his land (Exod. ix. 18-25), only more awful, and of such a character as to mark them as out of Nature's course and directly from God, here "cast" on the Roman earth, destroying its resources.

The *Second* Trumpet causes the fall of some great earthly power, symbolised by a burning mountain, such as the prophet describes the Babylonian kingdom to be (Jer. li. 25), cast into the sea, representing the tossing, changing condition of the nations (Chap. xvii. 15), in anarchy, without a head, resulting in great destruction of life and commerce. This will touch to the quick the world of progress, with its great mercantile and international pursuits.

The *Third* Trumpet marks the fall of some great dignitary, occupying a place of authority, either in what remains of apostate Christendom, or some new universal religion which has taken its place. Its name is Wormwood, and it poisons the water that men drink, the opposite of that tree at Marah (Exod. xv. 22-25), that sweetened them. For where the truth of the Cross and the love of it is rejected, a "strong delusion" will come from God (2 Thess. ii. 11), of which this fallen ecclesiastic apostate is the sign. How many smaller men of the same sort, while quickly flitting across the sky of Christendom, like meteor flashes, poison millions with their new theology and "doctrines of demons," before they fall from their status in the orthodox churches!

The *Fourth* Trumpet, which is the last of the first series—and the prelude to the Woe-Trumpets—brings complete anarchy among the governing powers, and a collapse of all rule, from the emperor to the petty magistrate, with a disruption of all social order, for the people want rule according to their own choice, and will get it. Here we see

THE BREAK UP OF GOVERNMENTS 95

how it ends. Some recent outbursts of lawlessness are an earnest of what this climax will be, only there will neither be military or navy to quell the rising. What a world it will be then! What a mercy that long before such a pass is reached, the whole of the saints of God of the outcalling of grace, with all the saved who have fallen asleep, will be at home in heaven, far above this turmoil and sea of trouble. Let it be remembered that the materials are already being got in order in the political, commercial, and religious world, out of which this will grow, and that the Word of God to His own, who are in danger of being mixed up and contaminated by intermingling with these corruptions is—"Come YE out from among them and be YE separate, saith the Lord" (2 Cor. vi. 17, R.V.).

CHAPTER IX.

SYNOPSIS:—The Fifth Trumpet brings its predicted Woe: A Fallen Star, an open Abyss, with Hell Smoke on Earth—Antichrist: His Origin, Character, Power, and Alliance with Hell—Apollyon and His Work—The Sixth Trumpet: The Second Woe, the Warrior Host, and the Ravages they make—Idolatry Continued, Rebellion and Defiance of God Increased.

A NEW development of Satanic agency appears, when the Fifth Trumpet is sounded throughout the Roman earth, especially that part of it which had been flooded with Gospel light, but being rejected had been withdrawn, leaving it in deeper darkness (John xii. 35). Here, God interferes judicially in the guilty scene. There is no mention of the appearance of the Lamb in these Trumpet blasts, for the time of mercy is past and these are Woe-judgments.

A Fallen Star. The Fifth Trumpet sounded reveals a "fallen Star"—whose fall has already been witnessed in Chap. viii. 10. Here he is seen as one that had *already fallen to earth*—some high dignitary in the moral heaven who had figured largely as a luminary among mankind, and earned for himself a position and a name. But he has now abandoned all that he professes to hold and teach, and comes out in his true character. Is this the Lucifer of Isa. xiv. 12-15, whose name means the Day-Star (R.V.), of whose coming Paul (2 Thess.

ii. 9-10), and John (1 John ii. 18: 2 John 7), foretell? That he will have a religious as well as a political career we know, and, as his many names and titles indicate, he will be an all-round individual, able to accommodate himself to all creeds, and able to play many parts in order to accomplish his ends, as the bulk of his forerunners who are busily engaged in Christendom, preparing his way and making ready a people to receive him, are doing now.

The Abyss. Here this scourge of God is allowed to hold for a time "the key of the pit of the abyss" (R.V.), that is authority over that infernal region. This "pit—or shaft—of the abyss," is not the lake of fire in which the devil and the lost have their final doom (Rev. xx. 15), but the place into which the demons prayed (Luke viii. 31) they might not be sent now. To this *abyss* the devil will be cast, and confined in it during the millennium (Rev. xx. 3). The place into which the souls of the lost go when they leave the body at death (Luke xvi. 23), is named *Hades*, or the Unseen, while the place in which the angels that sinned are confined is named *Tartarus*, and is described as dungeons or "pits of darkness" (2 Pet. ii. 5, R.V.). Evidently, by Divine permission, this fallen Being becomes the leader of hosts of demons, who emerge by this "shaft" or "well" in which they are now imprisoned, and resume their work on earth. These are not the spirits of the wicked dead, re-incarnate in living men, but demons who have been found on earth in "legions" (Mark v. 9), and can be called into localities by those who, as sorcerers, are in alliance with them, as in Spiritualism and Necromancy now.

Men on earth who desire to "communicate" with spirits now, will have their desire granted in full measure then. And they will learn, too, who they really are with whom they have been trafficking. The "smoke" that arises in such volumes from the nether regions, that it darkens the air, is hell smoke, not literal, but symbolic of delusions and deceivings spread over the earth by demons (I Tim. v. 1), in the form of evil doctrines, which, in the language of 2 Thess. ii. 11, 12, will "work error," causing the ungodly, who have cast off all profession of allegiance to God and Christ, to believe "THE lie."

The Locusts. The locust-like army which come out of this smoke are demons in some form, who go forth dealing intense torments, like scorpion stings upon men, especially Jews, who have not the seal of Chap. vii. upon them, but who have yielded themselves to Antichristian idolatry. The period in which these evil powers are permitted to inflict their vengeance is limited to "five months," and short as it is, the torment inflicted on living men on earth is so great that they seek death, but it flees from them (ver. 6). Over this host of tormentors is Abaddon, "the Destroyer," who inspires the demons who do his work, and he it is who gives the Antichrist his power, as we learn from Chap. xiii. 12, and lays out his work for him.

The *Sixth* Trumpet (verses 13-31), brings the Second Woe, which spreads over the whole of the Gentile earth. And this comes in answer to a Voice "from the Golden Altar which is before God," from which the prayers of saints on earth had ascended for Divine intervention. The "four angels" bound at the great river Euphrates—the boundary of the Roman Empire—are loosed, and these evil angels have under their control further powers of evil which here are let loose in retribution on the guilty world, already writhing in agony, and yet more hardened against God. This avenging host of fiends, numbering 200,000,000, from beyond the Euphrates, go forth dealing death to the "third part of men," wearing armour which protects themselves, and hurling death in such forms as savours of the torments of hell (ver. 18), already being felt upon earth. Yet men, spared from this awful doom, "repented not" of their sins —their "demon worship" and "sorceries," in defiance of God, and their "murders, fornications, and thefts," disregarding all human rights—but continued in impenitance and devilry, becoming more and more like the one whose gods they worship. Alas for the boasted culture and religion of the nations of Europe! Here is its inglorious end, gradually sinking downward and becoming more degraded, as God has depicted in Rom. i. 28-32.

CHAPTER X.

SYNOPSIS:—The Descending Angel—His Great Declaration—The Mystery of God Finished—The Little Book—John's Prophetic Ministry Resumed.

BETWEEN the sounding of the Sixth and Seventh Trumpets, there is a pause, during which events recorded in verses 1-7 occur. They are preparatory to the personal interference of the living Lord in the affairs of earth, and the establishment of His kingdom.

The Strong Angel described in ver. 1, is an uncreated Being, clothed in Divine Majesty, which can only be the Lord Himself. He comes down "*out of* heaven" as His proper sphere, where, as we know from Heb. viii. 1, He now sits on "the right hand of the Majesty" in the heavens, "clothed with a cloud," the emblem of glory veiling His person: "A rainbow upon His head," the emblem of covenanted mercy to the earth. His face "as the sun," His Divine Majesty as the coming King (Mal. iv. 2). In His hand "a little book," open and ready to read, the record of prophetic events unfulfilled, limited here to heaven's administration connected therewith. Planting His right foot on the sea, and His left on the earth, He asserts His right to both. His voice of majesty and might, like a lion's roar, brings terror among men, hardened as they are. And in response "seven thunders" utter their voices. The whole scene is of coming judgments, in which the Lord Jesus, after He has "risen up" from His present seat to begin His "strange work" of vengeance, will be the chief Actor, as the Lion of Judah, with voice of Power. But the time for this is not yet, nor can it be while "the Book" is closed (Luke iv. 20), and the "acceptable year of the Lord" continues its course. John was "about to write" the record of this, but was forbidden. These events, disclosed by the thunders, are not for the present: they are like those of Daniel, for "the time of the end" (Dan. xii. 9), which are not needed now. The solemn oath that there should be "no longer delay" (verses 5-7), that is in clearing the earth of rebellion and setting up His kingdom is here made by the Lord, and will not fail in fulfilment. The time has been long, but there has been no slackness. Divine longsuffering has been the cause (2 Pet. iii. 9), but now it is about to end.

The Mystery of God to be finished in the days of the voice of the seventh and last trumpet, is not the outcalling out the Church, as in Eph. iii. 9,—for this had been finished before the dead and living saints were caught up to meet the Lord in the moment of His coming "to the air" (1 Thess. iv. 17)—but the fulfilment of the first great promise of Gen. iii. 15, that Christ should finally triumph over Satan, and become Heir and Lord of all. This was known and testified of by "the prophets"— to whom the mystery of the Church, in union with

Christ, was a thing unknown (Eph. iii. 5),—but of His suffering and glories they testified (1 Pet. i. 11).

The voice from heaven bids John take from the angel's hand the open little book and eat it, an act which Jer. xv. 16 explains. For the Word of the Lord received and allowed to do its work in the soul produces effects (1 Thess. ii. 12), and gives joy or sorrow. The prophetic Word has its visions of coming glory, and its gathering clouds of woe, and the latter come first so far as earth is concerned. And this was to be the burden of John's message, not *to* but "OF peoples, and nations, and tongues, and many kings," and these especially who will have relations with Israel, God's earthly people, who are at this time coming into prominence as the people for whom He is acting in power, and through whom blessing is to be given to all nations when Jerusalem assumes her place as "the City of the Great King." It is to this grand climax that events are trending, and in anticipation of it the events of our next Chapter speak.

CHAPTER XI.

SYNOPSIS:—The Temple measured—The City trodden down—The Two Witnesses, their Power and Testimony—The Beast opposes and Kills them—Their Resurrection and Ascension to Heaven—The Earthquake—The Seventh Trumpet and the Announcement of the Kingdom.

THE scene of the Vision of this Chapter is in Jerusalem, the actual city, with a temple in its midst and worshippers therein. But it is not yet the Jerusalem that shall be, whose people "shall be all righteous," as the prophet speaks (Isa. lx. 21), for it is here the spiritual representation of "Sodom and Egypt" (ver. 8), morally degraded and ready for judgment. The temple here measured with its worshippers is evidently one built by the Jewish people, who have returned to their land still rejecting Christ, but observing Mosaic ritual. But among them are some godly ones, who worship the true God. "The Court" may symbolically point to the mass who are in coalition with Gentiles. These Gentiles are about to "tread under foot the holy city for forty-two months"—a period elsewhere given as 1,260 days (ver. 3), "a time, and times, and half a time" (Chap. xii. 14), otherwise three years and a half, the latter portion of the seventieth week (Dan ix. 24-27). During this period which will be "the time of Jacob's trouble" (Jer. xxx. 7), the Gentile powers who are against her will tread down her people "as mire in the streets" (Isa. x. 6). The return of the Jews, under the patronage of a great nation (Isa. xviii.) to Palestine, will make a covenant with the unnamed Kaiser of the confederated nations of the ten-kingdom Roman Empire, for seven years, or one prophetic week. During the first half of this week he flatters and favours them, but in the middle of the week he breaks his "covenant," which they discern to have been as an "agreement with hell" (Isa. xxviii. 15), and find themselves in his grip. He stops their national worship (Dan. ix. 27), forces idolatry upon them, and becomes their persecutor. The treading down of the city in ver. 1 is not in war, but in moral degradation, under the foot of the usurper.

The Two Witnesses. During this period of forty-two months, God raises up a testimony for His Name. Two witnessess clothed in sackcloth prophesy, sustained by Divine power in their testimony (Zech. iv. 1-6). They are made invincible to injury and death while they are needed, and some will doubtless receive their testimony of coming judgment, others, perhaps the majority, reject it, and "seek to injure" with their tongues as well as to "kill" with their weapons. The miraculous powers conferred upon them to protect themselves, and bring heaven's judgments on their foes, bring the position of Moses and Aaron, in Egypt, to mind (Exod. vii.-xii.), as do the signs they work. These signs have as their object not only the bringing awe on their enemies, but such conviction of these Israelites who had become apostate from God as in the days of Elijah, when God answered by fire.

THE TWO WITNESSES SLAIN

Their Martyrdom. When their testimony is finished, the Beast, who has been brought from the abyss by Satanic power, and who has already been exercising the authority conferred upon him throughout Christendom, turns his attention to those who in Jerusalem stand up for God and His claims. This he cannot allow, so he kills them in cold blood. His object is to silence every voice raised for God, whose place and worship he claims for himself. And so far had he succeeded in ensnaring the people of Jerusalem, and reducing them to moral degradation, that they actually leave the unburied bodies of these witnesses for God on their streets, for three and a half days, exposed to the gaze of the mocking, miscellaneous crowds who pass by, holding holiday over the triumphs of the Beast.

The triumph of the wicked is here as ever—short. If God does not prevent the Roman Beast from killing His witnesses—and let it here be remembered He did not prevent the same hostile power from crucifying the Lord of glory, of which surely there is a reminder in the designation of the place of their martyrdom, as the place "where also *their* Lord was crucified" (R.V)—He vindicates their mission, and manifests His approval of themselves by raising them from the dead, and calling them up to His holy heaven, to which they ascend "in the cloud" (comp. Acts i.9: 1 Thess. iv.17), in the sight of their enemies, which is a contrast to the resurrection of the Lord and that of His heavenly people.

Who Are They? Divers views are held and expressed as to who these two witnesses will be.

Most common perhaps is the thought that they will be *Enoch* and *Elijah*, the only two men of Old Testament time who reached heaven without tasting death. If this be correct, then as here seen they will yet share the common lot, "go the way of all the earth," and reach heaven through death and resurrection. Others see in them Moses and Elias, and we certainly find these names together in the last Chapter of Malachi (verses 4-6), in a connection which is suggestive. But "*two* witnesses" is a term frequently used for competent testimony (see Deut. xvii. 6: Acts i. 10), and may not be taken literally but as expressive of a full and effective testimony for God at this time. The earthquake that immediately follows with awful judgments, cause some to fear, but there is no record that their dread was followed by "repentance toward God," or anything more than as with Nebuchadnezzar, an acknowledgment that there is a God in heaven (Dan. ii. 2, 8, 47).

The Kingdom Announced. The sounding of the *Seventh* Trumpet brings the announcement from heaven, that "the world-kingdom of our Lord and of His Christ has come," and that its coming will be to the angry nations their last and deepest woe. But this is only yet in anticipation, so far as earth is concerned, for the Trumpets carry us on to the actual advent of the Lord in glory and judgment. But the bare announcement of it brings forth the worship of glorified saints in heaven, who ascribe, in a doxology, their praise.

CHAPTER XII.

SYNOPSIS:—A Woman Clothed with the Sun—The Manchild born to Rule—Caught up to Heaven—A Red Dragon Enemy on the Scene—War in Heaven—The Devil cast out—Celebrated in Heaven with Rejoicing—The Woman and her seed Persecuted.

CHAPTERS xii. to xiv. inclusive, form a special section of this Book, and one connected prophecy extending from the birth of Christ to the final judgment of the nations. Chapter xii., to which we now turn, is the most comprehensive chapter in Revelation, and a right understanding of its teaching will enable us to grasp the whole of the events to follow in their due order. The vision opens with a "great sign"—in heaven, "a woman clothed with the Sun." This woman is a symbol of Israel. Her royal dignity, governmental authority, twelve tribes, and subordinate ruling powers, are symbolised in the sun, moon, and stars, which were prophetically foreshadowed in Joseph's dream (Gen. xxxvii. 9). She is here seen according to God's thoughts, not on earth in failure, but as in heaven according to promise, under the new covenant in relation with God.

The Man-child. The Man-child is Christ, as Mic. v. 2: Isa. ix. 6, informs us—and ver. 5 confirms —Christ born to rule (Luke i. 31-33). But the words which are here primarily used of Christ personally, are applied also to His overcoming people in Rev. ii. 26, 27, so that what is predicted of the Head is true of the members—of Christ mystical, the Church, to be raised and glorified together with Him. The words of ver. 2, carry us back to the time before Christ's birth, which came through Israel (Rom. ix. 5 with Isa. lxvi. 7-10), in the way of sorrow, and is here mentioned to link it with the deeper sorrows upon which Israel is about to enter in the great tribulation.

The Red Dragon, seen also in "the heaven," is Satan, seen in all his malignant hatred of Christ, yet owned here as arch-ruler of the world (Eph. vi. 12)—a fact little believed now. Here he is seen grown into a huge monster, red with hatred, using the Roman power to execute his plans. Verse 4 was fulfilled at the birth of Christ personally in "Herod the King" (Matth. ii. 16), and it was "Pilate, the Governor," who signed the warrant for His death (Matth. xxvii. 26). And in each successive stage of the Church on earth, as one generation after another of the saints who compose "the Christ" mystical are born, persecution (Acts viii. 1: Rom. viii. 36) has raged. The long gap in which the Church is being formed is bridged over here, for the Chapter concerns Israel, and the rapture of the Man-child, Christ and His own, is only named incidentally to show where it comes in, in the chain of Divine purpose. "Caught up to God and to His throne," are words true alike of Christ Himself (Acts i. 9), and of His people (1 Thess. iv. 17). When God begins to deal again with Israel, the earthly

THE LAST CONFLICT IN HEAVEN

people, they become the objects of Satan's rage. The woman fleeing into the wilderness represents those of Israel who are true to God, during the period of Antichrist's false friendship, while others are cut off in judgment (Zech. xii. 1, 8, 9). These, God succours in the time of their distress, by providing a place of refuge during the three and a half years of Antichrist's cruel persecution, here stated to be 1,260 days, expressing the Divine care over its subjects day by day. This preserved company of Jewish witnesses seem to be those who ultimately stand on mount Zion, in Chap. xiv. 1, while those who are slain, appear standing on the sea of glass, in Chap. xv. 2.

War in Heaven. The scene that follows describes in the language of symbol, the clearing of the heavens of Satan and his hosts of wicked spirits, who now withstand and oppose the saints of God in their possession of their inheritance up there (Eph. vi. 12). Long has their power been felt by those who by faith would possess and enjoy that goodly land, but now the time has come for the word to be fulfilled, "the God of peace shall bruise Satan under *your* feet shortly" (Rom. xvi. 20). Under Christ, he has already had his head crushed (Gen. iii. 15), and his authority wrenched from Him (Heb. ii. 14), now the saints whom he hunted incessantly and withstood continuously, are to have the satisfaction of giving him the final stroke that will hurl him finally from his present place in the lower heavens. "Michael and his angels," who take the aggressive in the conflict, are named in Daniel x. 13, 20, 21, in connection with earthly kingdoms. But this scene is in heaven. Who this war-angel is, has been the subject of much speculation. "Michael, *the* archangel" (Jude 9), is said to stand up for the Jewish people (Dan. xii. 1), against spirit forces warring for their destruction. Here they fight directly with "the dragon and his angels," and the issue is their victory. If Christ and His glorified saints are described as mounted warriors, when they come forth into visible view, as in Chap. xix. 11, to execute judgment on armed hosts, led by their great chief on earth, why may they not appear in angelic form to conquer fallen angels, and hosts of wicked spirits in heaven? And who is charged to give the final blow to the devil, and cast him out, but the living Lord, with whom are associated His own? And so it is that those who were persecuted by these infernal hosts, and often sorely tried by their malignant wiles, share the final triumph of the Victorious Christ, in hurling them for ever from the place they have usurped in God's lower heavens.

The Devil on Earth. With all his titles heaped upon him: a Dragon as a monster in craft and cruelty, a Serpent in cunning and subtlety, "*the* Devil" as tempter and accuser, and "Satan," as adversary and enemy of Christ and His people, while of the whole habitable world he is "the Deceiver," this great Being of which so much is revealed in God's Book, is "cast into the earth," there for a season to carry on his malignant work. Here it may be noted that from this point onward his course is downward. Here he is cast from heaven to earth (ver. 9): at the beginning of the millennial reign he will be cast from the earth, and confined in the *abyss* for 1,000 years (Chap. xx. 3), at the close of which he will be consigned to the lake of fire (Chap. xx. 10)—his final doom.

A Doxology. The glorified saints in heaven celebrate the triumph in a doxology, "the salvation, the power, and the kingdom," all being named. The former now complete for body as well as soul (Rom. xiii. 11), the latter two always Christ's, now about to be manifested on earth as well as in heaven. The "accuser" has been removed, so that no longer can he malign before God those whom he had sought to tempt on earth. Those here named "our brethren" by the heavenly host, may refer to those who on earth had "overcome" during the period that intervened between the rapture of the heavenly company and the casting out of Satan, probably covered by the first half of the 70th week. The "Blood of the Lamb" gave them victory before God, and "the Word of their testimony," clear and fearless before men. Their devotion, too, is not forgotten, for it is known in heaven that "they loved not their lives unto death." The whole of the dwellers in heaven, saints and angels, are called to "rejoice" in the triumph. But what brings joy to heaven forebodes "Woe" on earth, for "the devil in great rage" has gone down to vent his anger on those whom God is now befriending there.

The Woman Persecuted (verses 13-17). His rage is turned against "the woman"—a remnant of God's Israel now in their land, probably in and around Jerusalem. But God is there, and bearing His own as on "eagle's wings," He finds a place of refuge "in the wilderness," into which they flee "from the face of the serpent"—the seducer, who, when he finds himself outwitted, casts a flood after them, which the sand of the desert swallows, symbolising the attitude of some earthly power toward the Jews who will befriend them. The persecution then rages against "the remnant of her seed," probably individuals found here and there who "keep the commandments of God, and have the testimony of Jesus"—two special marks, then as now, of a godly people. These described witnesses may be of those named in Daniel xii. 2, who "turn many to righteousness," poor, unknown, and unacknowledged here, but honoured by the King in the day of His glory with the name "My brethren" (Matth. xxv. 35), who in the time of their suffering were befriended by some, and neglected by others, among the nations. Thus the two lines—the heavenly and the earthly—are distinctly traced, the former with Christ in resurrection glory "in the midst of the throne," the latter on earth passing through fire and flood to find their place in the earthly kingdom. This distinction is the key to all that follows, as indeed it is to the entire teaching of this Book. The grouping of events in this great chapter carries us up to the point where the Jew comes into prominence as the object of Satan's hate, and when time and dates are again noted, for whenever the Jew and Jerusalem come into view, the broken thread of prophecy is resumed and its fulfilment proceeds.

CHAPTER XIII.

SYNOPSIS:—The Beast out of the Sea—The Revived Roman Empire and its Imperial Ruler—Ten Kingdoms with their Kings—The Claim to Universal Dominion and Worship—The Second Beast—The Antichrist: His Place, His Titles, His Work—The Doom of Both.

THE devil having been cast into earth, he finds instruments according to his will to effect his plans, and carry on his work of opposition to all that is of God there. The first and chief of these is here designated in ver. 1, as "The Beast." The word means a wild, ravenous beast. This is God's own symbol of the Roman Empire in Dan. vii. 1-8, and it is this empire in its yet future form, that is here brought into view. Its origin is said to be from "the sea" of tossing nations, exorcised by the power of Satan, who is here said to stand on the sand of the sea (ver. 1, R.V.), bringing the monster therefrom. The symbol means that the devil will use the suffrages of the masses to bring this once-great empire again into existence, in a ten-kingdom form, and their ten kings will, as Chap. xvii. 12 informs us, yield their subjection to one supreme Ruler over them all. This ruler will be a Gentile of great personal ability—coupled with Satanic power, for he is the devil's delegate and has all his authority. This Roman empire and its ruler are so completely identified in the Book of Revelation, that they bear the one name of "the Beast"—which term is applied to each, that is sometimes to the empire, sometimes to the emperor. The "seven heads" have reigned, the "ten horns" will yet reign together. They are Satan's instruments defying God, claiming Divine honours, persecuting His people, and both finally perish by direct judgment from heaven. The characteristics of this coming empire as given in ver. 2, combine the ferocity of all the four described in Daniel vii., and in addition its emperor accepts, direct from Satan, "his throne and great authority." Here we have a human being, endowed with the power of hell, to attract, deceive, and destroy at his will, And let it be remembered that God, who now in mercy restrains the power of Satan, will then withdraw His hand and let him have his way for a season, as men now wish. Verses 5-7 give the result. By pride, blasphemy, persecution, his power will extend over "every tribe and people and nation," and all except those whose names are written in the Lamb's Book of Life, *from* the world's foundation, a godly elect of Israel (Matt. xxiv. 22), will own this great blasphemer as their master, and worship him as their God. Having already noted in particular the course and end of this Roman Empire beast* I only remark that this resurrection-triumph of Satanic power will be a caricature of what God is about to do in bringing, as from the dead, His own earthly people into national existence, to be ruled over by His chosen

*See Lectures on the Book of Daniel, pages 71-75.

King, already raised from the dead as David's Seed (2 Tim. ii. 8: Luke i. 32, 33). It is the devil's travesty of the kingdom, his masterpiece imitation, which will first claim the world's admiration, then its worship. For his aim is to blot out God's Name from the earth, and claim His place for himself (2 Thess. ii. 4). And he will for a time succeed. Here all true saints having faith and endurance are to suffer, while they stand true to God, but they are not to fight in self-defence.

A Second Beast is seen in ver. 11, coming "out of the earth"—lamb-like, with a dragon's voice. This is the caricature of Christ, as Prophet and Priest, as the first beast is of Christ as King. This false Messiah is a *Jew*, who rules in Jerusalem as the representative of his emperor "THE Beast." He exercises all "his authority," and his work is to get the Jewish people and apostate Christendom to worship his imperial master. He is able to work miracles by Satan's power to attest his mission (2 Thess. ii. 9), as the Lord Jesus, in signs wrought by God (Acts ii. 22), had witness borne to His. He is able Satanically to bring fire from heaven, to make an image to the beast, cause it to breathe, and by these "signs" to gain greater numbers for the one he serves. In relation to Christendom he is THE Antichrist, spoken of as future, in 1 John ii. 22, a denier of the Son (2 John 7), "the lawless one" and "the man of sin" (2 Thess. ii. 4, 8). In relation to Israel he is the "one who will come in his own name," and by them will be received (John v. 43). As "the king," he will rule over the Jews in Palestine, make a seven years' covenant with them, pledge himself to protect and give them liberty of worship; but he breaks his covenant, forces idolatry upon them, bids all bear the mark of the Beast in forehead or hand, and refuses the right to buy or sell to all who refuse. These two confederates in evil act together, and together they perish (Rev. xix. 20). The dragon, the beast, and Antichrist—the trinity of hell—thus caricature the Father, Son, and Spirit. These two Beasts represent the *secular* and the *ecclesiastical* powers of their time. Clearly neither of them has yet appeared, for the Roman Empire ceased to exist in 476, A.D. Popery is not the answer to either, for it has waned, but these do not, until they perish suddenly and finally at the hand of the Lord. "The Beast" who personifies the revived Roman yet to be, is its eighth head, and as he has already lived as one of the seven, he will be a man raised from the dead by Satanic power.

666. The number of the Beast has been the subject of much speculation, and of many irreverent guesses. It is man's number *six*, God's is *seven*—completeness: this the devil cannot reach. It points to the fullest development of man's power inspired by Satan. Its full and true application will be known to the saints of God who will suffer for their faith in the terrible time of the Antichrist's rule, when death at man's hand, or damnation at God's, are the only alternatives. And there we leave it. Enough for us to know that "God is stronger than His foes," and that the final victory is not to be with the Adversary and his following, but with Christ and His saints. This is what these events are all clearly leading up to.

CHAPTER XIV.

SYNOPSIS:—The Lamb on Zion, the Earthly Company and their Song—The Everlasting Gospel—The Doom of Babylon announced—The Doom of the Beast-worshippers. The Blessed Dead—The Harvest and Vintage of the Earth.

TWO companies of redeemed ones, who come into existence after the present outcalling of the Church has been completed, appear in Chapter vii., one of Israel, the other from among the Gentiles. Here we have a third company, distinguished alike from "the elders" and the sufferers under the seals. They stand on mount Zion, the future seat of Divine government, upon which the Lord will "reign gloriously" (Isa. xxiv. 33), the place of Jehovah's choice (Psa. cxxxii. 13, 14), out from which will go forth the law (Isa. ii. 3), "beautiful for situation, the joy of the whole earth" (Psa. xlviii. 2), in the bright and blessed days to come. Clearly it is not in heaven but on earth they stand, but then both will be linked as John i. 51 tells us. These singers *stand* upon Zion, they *sing* before the throne, and none save themselves learn their song —for it is neither that of the heavenly people as in Chap. v., nor of the redeemed Gentiles as in Chap. vii. They are a preserved people who had not yielded to the Antichrist's claims, nor received his mark, during the period of the tribulation. They are undefiled, they follow the Lamb; they are bought, and no lie is found in their mouths, for they are blameless. All this points to them as a company of redeemed and faithful witnesses, for God and Christ, at a time when "all the world" was wondering after, and worshipping the beast, whose mark they bore, owning him their Lord and God, believing *the* lie (2 Thess. ii. 11). These clung to the truth, kept themselves separate, maintained a blameless life, and are now marked and deemed by God worthy of standing with the glorified Lamb, bearing His Father's Name on their foreheads, as His co-rulers in Zion. The scene is anticipative, for His actual reign has not yet begun. There are judgments great and awful yet to come, but this brief, bright glance of a praising and harping company beyond the clouds, tells that their warfare is accomplished. They are preserved and rewarded.

The Everlasting Gospel, which is here announced by an angel, is not the Gospel of God's grace (Acts xx. 24), and of our salvation (Eph. i. 13), as now proclaimed. It is a message to the mass of mankind (ver. 6), to "Fear God and give Him glory, for the hour of His judgment is come," which now we know it has not. (See John v. 25-28 for the two hours of Grace and Judgment.) Here, a recognition of God as Creator is claimed, in a time when this claim is denied by the worshippers of the Beast, and those who heed the message are named the "martyrs of Jesus" (Chap. xvii. 6), their death is reckoned as "in the Lord" (ver. 13), they are owned by Him, for they appear in resurrection glory in Rev. xx. 4, as co-reigning with Christ. So terrible will be the test in these times, so severe the "endurance of the saints," who, in face of death in its most dreadful forms, cling to "the commandments of God and the faith of Jesus," that a special "Blessed" is announced from heaven on all who thus "die in the Lord from henceforth"—being slain for their faith, from that point onward to the end. Rest now, and reward then is their portion.

Babylon's Fall is next announced from heaven here anticipately, and fully described in Chap. xvii.-xviii.. Her judgment pronounced in heaven here, is fulfilled there, with the human instruments of her destruction named, and the judgment of God fulfilled. Babel and Babylon are names, wherever found, in opposition to God. Their history begins in Gen. xi. 9, 10, and ends in Rev. xviii., first a political, last a religious corrupt confederacy.

The Beast-Worshippers' Doom. The words in which the judgment of high heaven is announced upon all who own the Beast, before or after Babylon's fall, is awful in the extreme, "in a loud Voice," too, so that none need fail to hear the warning. They are to "drink the wine of the wrath—the fury of God," unmixed with any mercy. And each is to be held responsible for his choice. No extenuating plea will be heard. Neutrality is impossible; it must be Christ or Antichrist: God or the devil. "If *any* man" now enter in by Christ, the Door, "he shall be saved" (John x. 9): here "if *any* one" owns the Beast as God, and receive His mark, which is the seal of his choice, "*he* shall be tormented in fire and brimstone," in hopeless, endless woe, "unto the ages of ages." There is no shadow of hope, no end of punishment, no alleviation of agony. Do some object? Do sinners reply against God's justice? They need not, for the punishment will be according to the guilt, and that guilt will be reckoned according to the dignity of the One against whom and whose Word it has been committed.

The Blessed Dead, in ver. 13, are, as has been noted, a special class, those who suffer martyrdom for their faith, to whom no hope of escape is held forth, and who have no promise such as Christians of the present age possess, that they "shall not all sleep" (1 Cor. xv. 51). To the Christian, death is as a "falling asleep," and to be "absent from the body" is to be "at home with the Lord" (2 Cor. v. 8, R.V.). Nevertheless death is not his proper hope, but to be "waiting for the Son from heaven."

The Harvest and Vintage describe two different actions of judgment, the former discriminative, the latter world-wide. In the harvest, angels are the reapers (Matth. xiii. 39), and they sever the wicked from the just. This may refer to the judgment of living nations as in Joel iii. 2, with the severance of sheep from goats in Matth. xxv. 40-45. The vintage is the whole earth ripe for unsparing vengeance. And the hour for that vengeance is now come (Isa. lxi. 2), the winepress of wrath is set up, and the Lord, as Son of Man and Judge, is seen, as in Isa. lxiii. 2-4, red in His apparel, treading that winepress. And so awful is the slaughter that the blood of the slain flows 1,600 furlongs—about 200 miles—reaching the "horses' bridles" in its depth. Thus the earth is cleared by judgment for blessing.

CHAPTERS XV. and XVI.

SYNOPSIS:—The Seven Last Plagues—The Harpers on the Sea of Glass—Their Song—The Angels with the Vials—The Wrath of God poured out—The Gathering of the Nations to Armageddon—Babylon's Fall—The Final Catastrophe.

THE two Chapters form one vision, and may be considered together. They set forth in strong and awful symbolical language the *last* of God's direct judgments from heaven upon men on earth—summed up in the words " in them is finished—completed—the wrath of God." "The wrath of *the Lamb*" will follow, when He appears in Person to overthrow the combined forces of evil, and to assume the government of the world, as the Second Man, the Last Adam. The Vials are borne by seven angels—as were the Trumpets (Chap. viii. 2)—and these they empty in due order by command of a "loud Voice from heaven."

The Martyred Harpists. Before these dire judgments proceed, we are allowed to have another glance of God's own, safely hid in His pavilion, beyond the judgment scene. These are the martyred saints who refused to own the Beast, and to receive his mark, and who, for their faith and faithfulness, were slain. Here they stand as victors, on "a sea of glass mingled with fire," clean like the former company of Chap. iv., their purification completed, while the "fire" here tells of the sufferings they endured, which had also purified their lives, while it "tried" (Dan. xii. 10) their faith. In their death they triumphed, now as victors they stand —not *sit* like the throned elders,—on that glassy sea in peace, while he who on earth had been their tormentor is having the first taste of the wrath of God. The song they sing is not the "new song" of Chap. v., but "of Moses the servant of God and of the Lamb." Victory through judgment was the theme of Moses' song (Exod. xv.), exaltation to the throne, through suffering unto death, is the song of the Lamb. And to Jehovah, as "Lord God Almighty, righteous and true" in all His ways, is the ascription given, for in His judgments as in His faithfulness to His own "all His ways are right." "King of saints"—is a bad rendering: the margin has "nations," the R.V. "ages." The Lord Jesus is never named King of saints, or King of the Church, but He is "King over all the earth" (Zech. xiii. 9), and "King of kings." And these nations are yet to own and "worship" before Him, when they behold His righteous acts (see Psa. ii. 4: Zech. xiv. 16: Psa. c.).

The Seven Vials. The temple vision seen by John in heaven, is in contrast to the words of Chap. xxi. 22, but no contradiction, for the age of the former is that of judgment, of the latter glory. Here the golden bowls, used in tabernacle and temple days for incense, are filled with wrath, and passed to angels, clad in purity and girdled in gold, expressing Divine holiness and faithfulness, by "the living ones," the glorified saints, who are in God's mind regarding His judgments. The temple filled with smoke is judgment, not incense, for there is no prayer to avert the doom of the ungodly now. The language used to describe the result of the pouring forth of the altar-bowls of God's wrath, is symbolic and not literal. The *First* produces a sore, like Egypt's plague, but is here both mental and physical—"evil" as well as "grevious," for men will have conscience as well as bodily pangs on earth and in hell. The *Second* brings blood and death on revolutionary peoples, who stagnate and become as "twice dead" (Jude 12), having broken all bonds between God and man. The *Third* takes life from all sources of vitality and prosperity, all becoming dead—morally, socially, politically. And in this judgment the "angel of the waters" concurs, saying that as "the blood of saints and prophets" have been freely shed, so these degraded murderers get "blood to drink," and in case any think this is too awful, he adds: "they are worthy"—and that is heaven's own verdict. The Lamb is *worthy* to reign: His enemies are *worthy* to be damned. The *Fourth* bowl poured on the sun, scorches and burns men, but their pains, instead of leading them to repentance toward God, incite them to "blaspheme His Name," which tells how hardened and incorrigible man is, and what he will be when left to his own will and way, led on by the devil. The *Fifth* bowl is emptied on the throne of the Beast, who, like Pharaoh of old, when the plagues of Egypt entered his palace, is at last reached, his kingdom is plunged in darkness, and his subjects smarting under the awful agonies and despair of that hour "gnawed their tongues for pain" (R.V.) in utterable distress. Yet their wills are unbroken, their hearts unmelted, for they "blaspheme the God of heaven"—the worst blasphemy of all, blaming Him for all their woe, "and repented not of their works." Those who idly argue for a "wider hope" in mercy beyond the present, or expect "a final restoration" of all through remedial agencies and punishments in hell, find no ground for either here. For these continue to glory in the very "works" on account of which the fiery wrath of a holy God is being poured upon them. The *Sixth* bowl dries up the great Euphrates—the mystic river of the East, first named in Eden (Gen. ii.), long the boundary of the Roman Empire, and yet to be the border of Israel's kingdom (Gen. xv. 18). The former Vials were poured on Israel's foes, here they reach to nations beyond. And this drying up of the Euphrates is in order that the way of the kings FROM the East "might be prepared." Along this way the hordes of Asia will sweep into Palestine, to join with those of the Beast in their final assault on the Lord Himself, and His covenant people then in Jerusalem. The power that gathers these "kings of the whole habitable earth," is described in verses 13, 14. It is Satanic, for it proceeds from the dragon's mouth; it is political, for it comes from the Beast; it is apostate and deceiving, for it comes from the Antichrist—the false prophet. "Unclean spirits"—"spirits of demons working signs," take possession of men—as they can do when God permits them—and these go forth as orators and miracle workers, "after the working of Satan" (2 Thess. ii. 9), luring on by deceit these warrior kings and their armies to Armageddon, the appointed gathering place, though not the scene of the fight—for there is no "battle of Armageddon" mentioned in the Word—thence to proceed in mass to Jerusalem, under the shadow of which they deliver their last great assault in the valley of Jehoshaphat. But it is "the war of the great day of God Almighty" now, and not any longer an affair of outposts. The issue can be in no doubt, for "God is stronger than His foes." The warning word of verse 15 to any of God's own who may like Lot in Sodom and Jehoshaphat with Ahab's army have got mixed among these enemies of high heaven, comes in solemnly here, for to them as to the world (1 Thess. v. 2, 3) the coming of the living Lord in judgment will be "as a thief," and they may in that hour be exposed and put to shame in the sight of the enemies of God. The *Seventh* Vial brings the final judgment. A voice out of the temple says, "It is done," and a cataclasm follows, which exceeds anything before seen. Thunders, lightnings, and earthquake demolish every system of government, disrupt all human relations, and bring a revolution such as this world has never known. "Babylon," the concentration of commercial and religious corruption, the defiler of nations, here falls, but the details of her character and doom are reserved to the two chapters that follow. And men now in their last extremity, under the power of God's wrath, show their adamant condition by still blaspheming God, because of His judgments.

CHAPTERS XVII. and XVIII.

SYNOPSIS:—Babel and "Babylon the Great"—Apostate Christendom in its Final Condition: its relation to God, to the State, and to the Nations—Her Worldly Grandeur and Luxury, Gorgeous Dress, Wine-cup of Abominations and Sorceries—Her Fall and Doom—The Wail of her Admirers, and the Hallelujahs of Heaven over her Judgment.

IN two instances already (Chap. xiv. 8 : xvi. 19), have we heard incidentally of Babylon's fall and doom. Here, in the way of recurrence, in two Chapters, we have a picture of this great and gorgeous system, under the symbols of a Woman and a City, first beheld in all her worldly greatness and grandeur, next as fallen, abandoned, and smitten by the Civil power which had supported her, and which was ruled by her, and finally by judgment, sudden and final, from God in high heaven. The word Babylon means *Confusion*, a mixture and mingling of that which God would have kept apart, leading on to a confederacy and organization in imitation of, and in opposition to, that which is of Him and from Him. Babel was its seed plot, begun by Nimrod, the first man, "mighty on earth," a leader and conqueror of men. The city and tower were his products, in open defiance of God, the first confederation of lawlessness earth saw, which ended in dire confusion and dispersion, Next, great Babylon, Nebuchadnezzar's city, on the Euphrates, was the opponent of Jerusalem, God's chosen city, having its temple and its god (Dan. i. 2), in imitation of His, to which as prizes of war God's temple-vessels were brought, to be desecrated and used in idol worship, impious revelry (Dan.v.5), and vile sorcery (Isa. xlvii. 9). Here, Babylon is a great, corrupt, ecclesiastical system, symbolized by a *Woman*, abandoned and unclean, a travesty of the chaste and pure (2 Cor. xi. 2) virgin bride of Christ, centred in a *City*, a vile caricature of God's New Jerusalem, the Holy City, from above (Rev. xxi. 2).

Apostate Christianity in its last form is that which produces Babylon. At the coming of the Lord to the air, all living Christians are taken from the world, and all the dead in Christ from their graves. Not one living born-again man or woman in mortal flesh will be left. But plenty of religious professors, preachers and people alike, with their churches and all the rest that goes to make up "religion." With nobody to trouble them by quoting "Thus saith the Lord," or calling attention to Christ's claims as Lord, things will progress rapidly on "downgrade" lines, and the great movement already in embryo, which has as its aim the fusion of all creeds and churches into ONE GREAT ORGANIZATION, including Catholics, Greeks, Anglicans, Lutherans, and all the smaller sects who are following hard on the heels of those from whom their founders seceded for the truth's sake, embracing in its scope all the "sacred and secular" affairs of religious mankind, allowing everybody to choose what is most to their taste in religion, so long as they do not insist that sinners need to be born again, and that there is no salvation save

through faith in the Christ who "died for our sins according to the Scriptures." THIS IS BABYLON.*
To all who lack spiritual vision she is "a mystery" (ver. 5), but to John and to the saint who is in "the secret of the Lord" that "mystery" is unlocked by the Spirit (ver. 7). And one has to be "in the wilderness" in separation from her, if he would see this gay woman and the scarlet coloured Beast that bears her. To be associated with either, or have personal interests involved, obscures the vision. For men are wonderfully quick in seeing what brings them gain or exaltation, but pur-blind where loss or the brand of the Cross may accrue from "more light." The details given in these chapters by the Spirit are so full and so intensely solemn, as here uttered in the language of sign and symbol, that they should be quietly read and prayerfully pondered rather than lectured on. All that I shall therefore do is, to briefly outline what I judge to be their import and message.

The Woman seen first sitting upon the "many waters," and later on a "scarlet coloured Beast," is the Apostate Church, rejected by Christ, now in open alliance with the world, supported by it, and for a season ruling both State and peoples religiously, clothed in attractive attire. This woman has abandoned all profession of loyalty to Christ, become a corruptress and a mother of such, in guilty alliance with kings and peoples (ver. 2), wearing the scarlet of the Beast and the Dragon. In relation to saints she is a murderess (ver. 6). Her name is blazoned on her forehead, for she knows no shame. Corruption is embodied in her.

*Note B.

The Beast is the political power, the revived Roman Empire in imperial greatness, godless and blasphemous, controlled by Satan. On this the woman sits. The two are distinct, although allied. The Beast comes from the abyss, and goes to destruction (ver. 8), and is described in its origin, course and end, in verses 9-10. Finally, the head of the Roman Empire, with his ten confederates, will join in throwing off the burden of this apostate Church, which has been ruling everything, and will first hate, then destroy her. In this they are at one, and this unity is given them by God although they know it not. In Chap. xviii. the doom of Babylon is directly traced to God, and is so announced by an angel. Stripped of her glory and wealth, she becomes after her downfall, a habitation of demons and a hold of unclean spirits (ver. 1). Her sins are named. In ver. 2 is a call to all God's people who may be found in any measure identified with her, to have no longer "fellowship in her sins," which even nominal adherence with an evil system or with a holder of evil doctrine is reckoned by God (2 John 11). Then "in one day" (ver. 8), in one mighty act likened to "a millstone cast into the sea" (ver. 21), Babylon sinks to rise no more. Lamentation is raised on all hands over her: by kings who trafficked with her, and merchants who were enriched by her commerce, which consisted of anything and everything from "gold and precious stones" to "slaves and souls of men"—the gold first, the souls last—on her trade list. All these wail over her doom. But heaven rejoices (ver. 20), and the "Hallelujahs" of the redeemed tell how her judgment is viewed up there.

CHAPTER XIX.

SYNOPSIS:—Joy in Heaven—The Marriage of the Lamb Announced—The Bride Prepared, Described, and Presented—The Bridal Guests—The Marriage Supper—Heaven Opened—The Conqueror and His Followers appear—The Great Event of the Future, Christ in Judicial Power—The Beast and False Prophet caught Alive and cast into the Lake of Fire—Their Armies Slain—The Supper of the Great God.

BEFORE the final judgment of living men at the hand of the Lord, when He returns in Person, is described, a vision of heavenly bliss, a scene of unparalleled glory is given. The heavenly host has rejoiced over the destruction of the false Church, and now these heavenly beings turn their thoughts to two grand events, namely the Marriage of the Lamb, followed by the descent of the Lord, as Victor and Judge, to clear the earth of its rebel leaders and their followers, in order that He may establish His kingdom and reign. A Voice comes from "the throne" calling for praise to "our God," which has an immediate response in a "Hallelujah," majestic as "the voice of many waters," loud and long as "strong thunders" rolling over the vast unnumbered multitude, saying: "Hallelujah, for the Lord our God, the Almighty, hath reigned"—hath taken His kingly power to reign. This had been anticipated in Chap. xi. 15: now it has come, and heaven is jubilant over it. The false Church has been destroyed, and the earth is about to be fully cleared of its oppressors.

The Marriage of the Lamb takes place within the heavens, between the Lord's coming *for* His saints and His coming *with* them. The Church is the Bride—not Israel. The Bride of the Lamb is the heavenly people, the Church for which He gave Himself on Calvary, who has been the special object of His service on the Father's throne since He returned there, and of the Spirit's care down here. And this espoused bride now glorified, looks upon Him in His beauty, seeing Him "as He is." She has been already presented as "the Church glorious" (Eph. v. 27), before all heaven. She has been there amid heavenly scenes, while judgments, dire and awful, have swept the earth which once as a pilgrim she trod, and already heaven has become her robing room for this auspicious day of her public union with the Lamb, before heaven's wondering throng of principalities and powers. And she has "made herself ready." The review of the lives and service of individual saints is over: the rewards of the judgment-seat have been given. She is arrayed in lustrous linen robes, which are said to be the righteousnesses, "or righteous acts of saints," done, but generally unrecognised or misrepresented on earth, but now estimated at their true value and recompensed in heaven. In these she stands arrayed—not for acceptance, for that is found in Christ's preciousness alone (1 Pet. ii. 7) —but "given" by Him who knew what it cost her to maintain the undefiled walk and the unspotted garments (Rev. iii. 4, 5), in earthly years.

The Guests. John is told to write "Blessed are they who are called to the marriage supper of the Lamb." This is not the Bride, but the guests, "the friends of the bridegroom," to whom John the Baptist likens himself in John iii. 29. Saints of earlier and later dispensations will be there, but the Bride is unique. Over her the Bridegroom rejoices with a peculiar joy (Jude 24), and her joy in Him is full (John xv. 11).

The Gathering Armies. While the Lamb is thus celebrating His marriage within the heavens, amid the unbounded joy of celestial hosts, scenes of another sort are transpiring down on the earth, where the devil, the beast, and Antichrist, have it all their own way. Hordes from the far East, of which we heard in Chap. xvi. 14, gathered instrumentally by demons, but in judicial act by God (ver. 16), for He it is who assemblies "the nations and kingdoms to pour upon them His indignation" (Zeph. iii. 8), are already in Palestine, and have begun their grand assault on Jerusalem. Already awful horrors have been enacted within its walls, half of its people are led captives, and its fall seems imminent. But the hour of its deliverance is come, "For in that day shall the Lord of Hosts defend the inhabitants of Jerusalem" (Zech. xii. 8). Out on the plain of Megiddo (Armageddon), the beast and his ten subordinate kings, with the whole chivalry of Europe, are gathering for the last great offensive. "It is the battle of the great day of God Almighty." Never before has earth witnessed such a sight. Inflated by pride, driven on by demons, the Emperor is there in person, with his prime helper and adviser, the false prophet, the Antichrist, at his side. When lo! in a moment, the blue heavens above part asunder, and the living Lord, the despised and rejected Nazarene, last seen by the world on a felon's cross, appears, not in lowly form, but clothed with majesty. This is "the Revelation of Jesus Christ," His epiphany to the world, the scoffer's jest, and the hypocrite's fear. Yes, it is He, the Man of Calvary, from the throne of God at last, invested with power to tread down His foes, give deliverance to His own, and bring the world at last into subjection to God.

The Victor and His Following. Heaven is opened to the Seer, and a white horse, the symbol of Victory, with One seated called "Faithful and True," who is to judge and conquer. His eyes "as a flame of fire" search and penetrate all; nothing is hid from His gaze. He wears on His head "many diadems," regal crowns—once on the false one's brow (Chap. xiii. 1)—which are His by right, for all authority is His. His incommunicable Name proclaims Him Divine, "the Word of God"—mighty once to create, here to judge. "His Vesture dipped in blood," tells of enemies already fallen (Isa. lxiii. 1, 2). "The Armies in heaven" following Him are the glorified saints, all of them here viewed as the companions of the Victor, going forth to judge. This is the fulfilment of Enoch's prophecy, "Behold, the Lord cometh with ten thousands of His saints to execute judgment" (Jude 14, 15). Angels, too, swell the train (Matth. xxv. 31 : 2 Thess. i. 7). He alone is *the* Warrior and has the "sharp sword," which smites the nations, and He too "shall govern them with a rod of iron" (Psa. ii.), breaking their lawlessness, and subjecting them by judgment to His sceptre, for He is "King of kings and Lord of lords." A sword to pierce, a rod to rule, a winepress to tread, all tell of judgment, the last of a vengeance which He administers alone (Isa. lxiii. 3).

The Great Supper. In striking contrast to "the marriage supper of the Lamb," to which honoured guests are "called" in heaven, an angel here summons ravenous fowls to eat the flesh of kings, and captains, and warriors, for there is no doubt in heaven as to the issue. Such will be the inglorious end of the greatest army this world has ever seen! And now for the battle scene! The clash of arms as in earthly warfare is unheard.

The Leaders Caught. As once the glory of the Lord shone round Saul, the persecutor, casting him to the ground, so these rebel hosts wither before "the brightness of His coming" (2 Thess. ii. 8). The two leaders "the Beast and the False Prophet"—found up to the last at the side of his chief—are taken alive, red handed in their guilt, and without trial or mercy, cast into the lake of fire, its first tenants from earth, to endure its torments a thousand years before any other human being. Thus as two men from earth, Enoch and Elijah, eminent for their faithfulness, went to heaven without tasting death, so here the two greatest enemies of God and His people this earth will ever see are consigned alive to the burning lake to endure its unspeakable agonies. "The rest were slain" not with material sword, but with "the breath of His mouth."

CHAPTER XX.

SYNOPSIS: — The Binding of Satan — "The Thousand Years"—Reign of Christ and His Saints—The First Resurrection—The Millennial Kingdom—Satan's Loosing and Last Rebellion—Gog and Magog—The Devil's Final Doom—The Great White Throne—The Dead Raised and Judged—The Last Assize—The Lake of Fire.

FROM Chap. xix. 11 to Chap. xxi. 8, a consecutive order of events is traced, extending from the appearing of the Lord in His Warrior judgment to the Eternal State. The first scenes in this great drama have already passed before the Seer, the rest are recorded in our Chapter.

Satan Bound. The last and greatest enemy of mankind, as he was the first, is next dealt with. His expulsion from heaven was noted in Chap. xii. 7-13; his presence and work on earth has been witnessed during the interval. Now an Angel from heaven, with the key of the abyss, and bearing a chain, lays hold on the great mysterious Being, who has been the originator of all earth's woe, destroying as a dragon, deceiving as a serpent, and chains him up in the bottomless pit—the *abyss*, out from which he had called the Beast, to do his work on earth. Into this *abyss* he is now thrust himself, his liberty taken from him, his power restrained, his evil influence as "prince of this world" and "god of this age," so long exercised over men, brought summarily to an end. But his final doom is not yet. Here he is locked and sealed into the pit, while the earth enjoys its sabbath rest, and its true King reigns over it in peace.

A Thousand Years—a period six times named in these verses, is that from which the word *Millennium* comes, and this term has come to be used as the designation of the period of Christ's reign. And here, too, we learn that there are some who will reign with Him, seated on thrones, with judgment given them. The hour for this great kingdom, spoken of by prophets, sung by psalmists, and looked for by godly ones of all ages, has actually come. Earth's rightful King is on its throne: the reed, the purple, and the crown of thorns are gone for ever. The Victor's Crown of gold has been on His brow, on the Father's throne: now the Kingly diadem is on His head, and He is seated on His own throne. And some are seated with Him? Who are they? His heavenly people had the promise from His own lips in glory, that they who overcame would sit with Him there (Rev. iii. 21). And earlier in the days of their militancy, the saints were told that those who suffered here would reign with Him hereafter (2 Tim. ii. 12). These include all who have been raised and changed at Christ's coming, the saints of former ages as well as the Church. They are here seen reigning as kings with Christ. But there are others, two groups of them too, consisting of saints whose conversion and testimony had been *after* the Church's call was complete. First, are those who had lost their lives for the testimony of Jesus, and the Word of God

(R.V.), already named in Chap. vi. 9-11: all of whom were martyrs. Here they are seen raised and reigning. Then there are those who had stood true to God, during the reign of the Beast, refusing his mark and sharing a martyr's death. These, raised *after* the first group of 1 Thess. iv. 16, possibly after the appearing of the Lord, are included in "the first resurrection." And this first resurrection includes (1) Christ, its First-fruits ,(2) afterwards they that are Christ's at His coming, (3) these martyred saints, each being a resurrection from, or out from the dead, leaving others not raised. And so we learn from verse 5: "But the rest of the dead lived not again until the thousand years were finished." The wicked dead, whose souls are in Hades, will lie in their graves undisturbed during the thousand years of glory. Then *all* of them, from Cain onward, rise together for judgment (John v. 28). The first resurrection includes *all* saints, and all who share it are "blessed" and "holy;" priests in communion with God, kings in government with Christ. The theory of a general, simultaneous resurrection of all mankind, has no foundation in the Word of God.

The Millennium. Descriptive details of the reign of Christ and His saints are not given here. Other Scriptures informs us of its heavenly and earthly aspects, and tell, in glowing words, its characteristics and its blessing. Earth will have its sabbath, creation its deliverance, the brute creation their release from the curse, and man on earth his last trial. In innocence, without law, under law, in a kingdom, under grace, he has failed and sinned. Now under perfect government, with glory all around, he repeats the story, which proves his utter ruin, apart from redemption and regeneration. With Satan bound, nothing to tempt, everything in his favour, those who are born during the millennium, if not born again—as all will not be—will, whenever they get the opportunity, show whose they are. They dare not during Christ's reign of righteousness, so they yield a "feigned obedience" (Psa. xviii. 44), to the rod—for it would mean their immediate death (Isa. lxv. 20) to rebel, but their chance at length comes, and they take it.

Satan Loosed (verses 7-10), for "a little season" (ver. 3), goes forth to resume his former work of deceiving the nations, and succeeds so well that he gathers from all quarters a following so large that it is likened to "the sand of the sea shore," crowding around Jerusalem, where Christ has His throne, and above which hovers the heavenly city, with its glory enlightening it. It is Satan's last attempt, and it fails. There is no need for the reigning Christ or His saints to intervene. God in high heaven, "over all," takes up the assault. "Fire came down from God, out of heaven, and devoured them," in swift overwhelming judgment, and thus the wicked are for ever extinct on this earth.

His Final Doom. The only survivor is the devil. His satellites, the Beast and Antichrist, are already in the lake of fire, and into that lake the personal devil, the arch-deceiver, whose doom God pronounced in Eden, is now cast, to endure its unending torments, not to reign there, as sages dream and poets sing, but to remember in bitter remorse his downward course, from an archangel's throne to the lowest depths of degradation and doom, himself the most abject being there.

The Great White Throne, the resurrection and judgment of the dead, and the final destiny of the ungodly, close this great Chapter. We have seen the throne of the King, here it is that of the Son of Man. He sits thereon, and all judgment is committed to Him there (John v. 27). He has already judged the living, now He is to judge the dead. From before His face the earth and heavens flee, no refuge or hiding-place is left, time ceases and eternity begins. "The dead, small and great, stand before the throne" (R.V.)—not before God, for Him they see not. This is the resurrection of "the dead"—spiritually dead—of the unjust (Acts xxiv. 15). What a concourse from land and sea, from Death and Hades, the former yielding the body, the latter the soul—from every land, of every rank, of every age, all there to hear from the righteous Judge, whose open books bears full testimony to each one's deeds, His verdict on their works. "The Book of Life," too, is opened, and shows that no name in all that vast throng is there, for however much they differed in earthly years in character and conduct, all rejected God's "free gift of life eternal in Christ Jesus" (Rom. vi. 23). Death and Hades, now empty and done with, are cast into the lake of fire. There, also, all whose names are not in Life's Book are cast, there to remain. And this lake of fire is named "the second death," which is not extinction, nor annihilation, nor can it be restitution but hopeless, endless woe.

CHAPTERS XXI. and XXII.

SYNOPSIS:—The New Heaven and Earth—The New Jerusalem—The Tabernacle of God with Men—The Eternal State—The Bride of the Lamb—The Holy Jerusalem Described—The River and Tree of Life—The Bliss of the Redeemed—The Last Words.

THESE Chapters may be best considered together. They present the Bride of the Lamb, first and briefly in her relation to the Eternal State, then in the way of recurrence she is more fully described in her relation to millennial times. Chap. xxi. 1-8, with the brief glimpses in 1 Cor. x. 24-28: 2 Pet. iii. 13: Eph. iii. 21, give us all that God has seen fit to reveal of the eternal state.

The New Heaven and Earth, in all their perfection and beauty, fresh from the hand of God, appear, after the former had passed away. In them righteousness will *dwell* (2 Pet. iii. 13), sin will never enter, sorrow will never be known there. "No more sea" to divide and sunder as now, gives ample space on the new earth for all its holy dwellers, God has His tabernacle "*with* men" (R.V.). He makes His abode with them; He, Himself, in all His revealed character as Light and Love, is their God, known, enjoyed, adored.

The Holy City is symbolic of the Bride of the Lamb in her glorified state—"New Jerusalem"—

not the earthly city as described in Isa. lx., nor the "heavenly Jerusalem" of Heb. xi. 10: xii. 22—which is a fixed locality, the home of all the heavenly people, but the glorified saints in their unity, each individual " a house" (2 Cor. v. 3), in the vast, mystic city, here seen as "coming out of heaven" her home, "from God" her Maker, "prepared as a bride," fresh in immortal youth, after a thousand years, for in her there can be no decay. "All things new" surround her, for "the former things have passed away." The kingdom has been delivered up by the Son, and God is "all in all," the Source of bliss to all, Alpha and Omega, Originator and End of all, the Fountain of Life to all. The final doom of the lost is stated in few but awful words, eight groups, including all classes, being named as having their part in the lake of fire, in fixed and hopeless misery. And this is in the eternal state. From verse 10 to Chap. xxii. 5, is

The City Described in her millennial splendour as the Lamb's Bride, associated with Him, having "the glory of God," her light or lustre being like a jasper stone, through which that glory shines, "crystallising" all upon which it falls. This symbol city is suspended between heaven and earth, its transparent walls shedding their rays upon the earthly Jerusalem, whose "light" it is (Isa. lxi. 1), and in that light the "nations" walk. It has "no temple," for God is known to all. It needs no sun, for the Lamb is its lamp, God's glory seen in Him illumines all. It is "pure gold"—all Divine: its streets as transparent glass, reflecting the walk of all its righteous people. It is the seat of Divine government, for Christ and His people are ruling there. Twelve gates express its earthly administration, which will be exercised by the saints, the twelve apostles being over the tribes of Israel (Matth. xix. 28). Gates of pearl, set in the jasper wall, at which angels wait as servants without, tell its freedom. This golden city, all of God and filled with glory, is the perfection of all God's works, the dispenser of His richest blessings to men. The "river of water of life," symbol of freshness, fulness, gladness: the "tree of life" on either side of its flow, tells of life abundant, never to be lost, its fruits for satisfaction to the glorified, its leaves for healing to the nations. Amid these eternal beauties, the "Lamb is all the glory," and His servants "see His face" as they serve Him in unwearying energy.

Last Words. After describing the home and bliss of His own, and their eternal portion with Himself in glory, He thrice repeats His old time promise (John xiv. 3), to come Himself and receive from the world His own. For this is their proper hope, and He Himself is the Lover of their hearts. And here He adds the word "quickly," with a final message to all. First (ver. 7), to keep the sayings of this Book, following on as its light leads. This will be remembered when He comes. To His servants (ver. 12), He will bring rewards for faithful service here. The last word is simply "Surely I come quickly" (ver. 20). And there is no promise added, for none is needed. It is "Himself" (1 Thess. iv. 16), the Lord and Lover of the saint, the Bridegroom of the Church, who is coming! Coming as "the Bright and Morning Star," harbinger of the glorious day. That word—the very last from heaven, awakes a chord, and John personally, and for the Church representatively, replies. "Amen, Come, Lord Jesus." May this be our attitude, and this our heart's response, till we hear His gathering "shout," and rise to meet Him in the air.

NOTES.

NOTE A.—Historic interpreters, such as Fleming, Cumming, Barnes, Elliott, Farrar, Guinness, find the symbols of Chaps. vi. to viii. answered in events of the last two thousand years, and hold them to be already past, whereas they are said by the Lord to belong to "the things which shall be *after these*"—that is, after the present dispensation is past. And they find in the opening of the Seals, the conquests of Marcus Aureleus, the edicts of heathen men, the reign of Constantine, and such like: in the Trumpets, the invasions of Goths, Vandals, Huns, and Saracens, and the Turks investiture of Constantinople. In Chaps. x.-xvi. they see Reformation times, and find in the woman the Papacy, the Beast the clergy, Antichrist the Pope, and so on. But this is not exposition, but supposition, and necessitates the reader of the Book of Revelation to be versed in all the world's lore and history, in order to understand it.

NOTE B.—Some reverent readers of the Word see in this name a literal city, yet to be built on the Euphrates. Such say, the predictions of her complete overthrow (see Isa. xiii.) have not yet been fulfilled, and that her decay from neglect through generations is not her final judgment from heaven. Present activity in all that region points to the probability of a return of commercial greatness to lands of the East in which the race was cradled. And there is nothing known to us to prevent the revival of Babylon as an actual city and centre of earthly greatness. But the symbolic city of Rev. xviii. represents something far wider and greater than can be localised. It is a world-wide system of corruption, spreading its influence among all nations.

1. Where in Revelation does the resurrection and rapture to heaven of the Church come in? Symbolically in Chap. iv. 1, probably in Chap. xii. 5 also. But we do not look for repetition of what is fully taught in the Epistles in Revelation. It is concerned with events hitherto unrevealed.

2. Will *all* the saved on earth be changed and removed when the Lord comes, or only waiting and watching saints? "*They that are Christ's at His coming*" (1 Cor. xv. 23). And "*We which are alive and remain*" (1 Thess. iv. 17), leave no doubt that the grave and the earth will be emptied of saints when Christ comes. And the words of 1 Thess. v. 10, R.V. are definite, that spiritual slumber will *not* cause any to be left.

3. When and where is Christ's judgment seat? In heaven, after His coming *for* His saints and before His coming *with* them (2 Cor. v. 6-10). They will then be in glorified bodies, like Christ, with Christ, and will know as they are known. The saints will have received their rewards before the marriage of the Lamb (see Rev. xix. 8, R.V.).

4. Are the signs named in Matth. xxiv. to be expected before the Lord comes? Yes, before His coming to earth as Son of Man and Judge, to deliver Israel and rid the world of evildoers. But this is not the Christian's hope. It is His coming as Son of God to the air (1 Thess. iv. 15, 16). No signs precede this.

5. Will the Jews' return to Palestine be of a spiritual character? Not at first. The Zionist movement is political, its object is to gain Palestine for the Jew. Those who return will do so in unbelief, join themselves to the Gentiles, and become rich. But their time of trouble awaits them there.

6. Does the Year-day principle of interpretation of Scripture help to a right understanding of prophecy? Do the 1260 days of Rev. xii. 6 mean years? By no sound canon of interpretation can this be shown. The same period is named, "time, times, and half a time" (ver. 14, with Dan. vii. 25), three and a half years, and 42 months (Rev. xi. 21), both referring to the latter half of Daniel's 70th week. The Year-day theory is tradition.

7. When is the one taken, the other left? (Matth. xxiv. 40, 41). Is it when Christ comes? The context shows it is at the coming of the Son of Man: one is taken away in judgment, the other left for blessing on the earth. At His coming to the air, it will be just the reverse.